MW00353933

California State
Notary Public:
A Guide and Reference Manual

Chris Morgan

Fifth Edition 2017

For additional copies or bulk purchases of this training and reference manual
please contact

The Notary Public Institute
849-C Almar Avenue, Unit #450
Santa Cruz, CA 95060

www.thenotarypublicinstitute.com

Copyright © 2011 - 2017 by Chris Morgan

This guide and reference manual is being sold with the understanding that the publisher/author are NOT rendering legal, accounting or any other professional services. If legal or other professional assistance is needed, the services of a competent professional should be sought.

No part of this publication may be reproduced or transmitted in any form or by any means, electronic or mechanical, including photocopying, recording or information storage and retrieval by a system now known or to be invented without the written permission of the author.

Fifth printing 2017
Printed in the United States of America

FOREWARD

At some point in our lives, each and every one of us has been or may be required to take an examination for validation, admission, qualification, certification, or licensure. The process of preparing for such an examination can often be overwhelming, terrifying, and in some cases, paralyzing. Some of the following thoughts may come to mind as you start your preparation:

- Where do I start?

- How in the world am I going to pass?

- I don't know what I'm doing?

- Does anyone have a straight forward simple to follow solution for me?

If you have any of these thoughts, you have come to the right place.

The Notary Public Institute was created to help prepare individuals that are vying for a state appointment as a new or renewing notary public. The training provided by the Notary Public Institute is meant to assist the student in his/her preparation for the California state notary public examination. A successful preparation requires that the reader completes the reading assignments, study and answer all examination preparation questions, and actively participates in the course. To successfully complete all the exercises contained in this workbook and meet the state requirements takes a commitment on the part of the student of six hours for new notaries or three hours for renewing notaries. Based on the assumption that you read all required sections and complete all practice examination questions, your preparation will be _more_ than adequate for you to easily pass the state examination with confidence.

In closing, this reference and guidebook, is an important factor in helping you to pass your exam and to go on to function, with confidence, as a California State Notary Public. The true calibration of my success as an author will be determined by your success in passing the state exam and operating competently as a notary.

Thank you for your service as a California State Notary Public.

Chris Morgan
Owner - Instructor

Contents

Chapter 1 - Becoming A Notary

Chapter 4 - The Notarial Journal and Tools of the Trade

Chapter 5 - Notary Shield Protecting Yourself

Chapter 6 - Government Codes

Appendices

Introduction

Notary History

In early history the ability to read and write as well as the widespread use of paper were not very prevalent. Public officials, known as Notaries, were employed to transcribe documents into writing and keep the documents in a safe place. These documents generally consisted of agreements that individuals wanted to create a public record of or various documents and wills that were to be kept in full legal force and effect. The term "full legal force and effect" is simply used as a clarifying phrase to reinforce the notion that a negotiated contract binds two parties to a written document.

Those individuals that were unable to write used a disk that was made out of clay or metal, called a "private seal". On this disk they would engrave a distinctive design or coat of arms that served as a signature. A sticky hot wax was dripped onto the paper at the end of the document, and the "private seal" was impressed into the wax. From this act comes today's definition of the verb "seal," which means to "make secure" or "enclose" an object.

In the following decades and centuries many more people learned to read and write. This growth in our literacy when combined with the mechanization of papermaking resulted in an increase in the supply of paper.

The growth in the number of people that were capable of reading and writing resulted in the rapid growth in literacy in states enacting laws to govern various forms of agreements. As the work of drawing up laws, contracts, and wills became more complicated, duties that had once been performed by notaries public were taken over by attorneys. Notaries were then left with non-legal (ministerial) functions, as they are today. The notary testified in writing as to the identity of the person(s) who signed and/or affixed their private seal to the agreement. The notary witnessed the signing of the agreement and took the acknowledgment of the parties. For the agreement to be in effect; the notary took all necessary precautions to ensure that the agreement was properly sealed (in the sense of "made secure") so that it could not be tampered with. Finally, the notary was sometimes held responsible for keeping and preserving the original document in a safe place.

In the United States during our early colonial days, the colonists had little need for the services provided by a Notary Public. The colonists were more interested in developing the country. Most

FAST FACTS:

Individuals that were unable to write used a disk that was made out of clay or metal called a "private seal."

agreements for the purchase and sale of land were made public in open court. The buyer and seller met in front of an official, such as a judge, to advise him of their intention to make an agreement. Judges would make and keep a record of their agreement, secure the document, and in many cases store the official document.

However, the eventual increase in trade between the Colonies and Europe pointed out the need for an official of *high moral character*, such as the Notary Public, who could witness, as well as draw up simple agreements for the purchase and sale of merchandise. Colonists used a "bill of exchange" to pay for merchandise that was received from Europe.

The Constitution of the United States left the responsibility for the enactment of notary laws to the individual states. Therefore, each state developed notary laws based on the commercial interests, business needs, and the customs of its citizens.

Notaries were also empowered at this time to take oaths and affidavits. These differed from depositions in that they were not always used in connection with court proceedings. Affidavits were required for such documents as creditor's bills, publication of delinquent tax lists, homestead claims, government claims for mineral lands, and government back pay and pensions.

As the states were surveyed and property became more valuable, written agreements were needed for the conveyance or buying and selling of land. Notaries public were authorized to take the acknowledgments of deeds, conveyances of land, mortgages, and other documents relating to real estate. It became the notary's duty to identify the parties, witness their signatures (and private seals in some cases), obtain the individual's acknowledgment that the agreement be in full force and effect, and affix his/her official notary seal and official signature to the certificate of acknowledgment.

In the 19th century, some of the states permitted or required the person whose signature was being notarized to use a private seal in lieu of or in addition to his/her signature on a document. If the person was unable to write, he/she was permitted to make an "X" as their mark or signature. Some states enacted laws prescribing the acknowledgment forms to be used by the notary when a person signed their name with an "X". The private seal in that time was often called a "scroll seal" or "scrawl" and consisted of the written word "seal" or the letters "L.S." enclosed in loops or parentheses. The form varied according to the handwriting of the

FAST FACTS:

If a person was unable to write, he/she was permitted to make an "X" as their mark or signature.

person whose signature was being notarized. The metal seal embosser as we know it today was not yet in use either as a private seal or an official notarial seal.

Until the office of the Recorder of Public Documents was established in the U.S, good business practice and often state law provided that the notary keep a record book or register of his/her acknowledgments, or proofs of acknowledgments of deeds as well as some of his other notarial acts. It should be noted that the notary may often have kept the original document in his/her files and thus it was not necessary to record the details of the notarization in his/her record book. Most all states enacted laws requiring that a notary make a certified copy of all documents in his/her records for anyone upon payment of the proper fee to see. Because public recorders were few, and machines for making copies of documents did not exist, the notarial record book served a very different purpose than it does today.

Also, the country of origin of the citizens of a state had an important influence on the kind of notary laws that were enacted in that particular state. Those states whose inhabitants originally came from England tended to follow the English laws and customs in connection with the enactment of laws and statutes governing notaries public. The customs and laws of the country of their origin also influenced those states whose citizens came from other countries. For example, the French influences on Louisiana notarial laws, even today, enable notaries in Louisiana to perform many duties that in most other states are considered practicing law.

In preparation for the writing of this book, I interviewed many people and asked them to explain the duties, functions and authority of a California notary. The answers ran from vague responses to outright "I don't know". Most people were somewhere in the middle with answers like "they're people that legalize important papers" and "they're people that stamp and sign important papers". These responses are a step in the right direction, but they clearly don't go far enough.

So what is a notary public now at the dawn of the 21st Century? *A notary is an individual of proven integrity that has been appointed by the Secretary of State to serve as a state official functioning as an impartial witness.* Notaries are technically **ministerial officials**, which is different from that of judicial officials. Ministerial officials have very little discretion and are required to follow written rules as they carry out their official duties.

FAST FACTS:

A notary is an individual of proven integrity that has been appointed by the California Secretary of State to serve as a public official functioning as an impartial witness.

To conclude, the factors that have affected the enactment of notary laws in the states vary according to the business needs of the community, their business practice customs, and the country of origin of the citizens. In many cases, notary laws were not enacted until it proved necessary to control improper practices. States that had little need for notaries passed a minimum of notary laws while others enacted extensive notary laws out of necessity.

FAST FACTS:

A deposition is a witness' out of court testimony that is reduced to writing for later use in court or for discovery purposes.

What's New for 2017?

The following three changes were made to California State Notary law and went into effect on January 1, 2017.

Acceptable Identification:

Civil Code section 1185 was amended to change the types of acceptable identification used for proof of identity by adding a valid passport from the person's country of citizenship, a valid consular identification document issued by the consulate from the person's country of citizenship and an identification card issued by a federally recognized tribal government to the list of acceptable documents if the identification is current or has been issued within the last 5 years, contains a photograph and description of the person named on it, is signed by the person, and bears a serial or other identifying number.

Government Code sections 6107, 8205, 8206, 8213, and 8213.5 were amended to require a person taking and subscribing the notary public's oath of office before a county clerk to present one of the following forms of identification:

- An identification card or driver's license issued by the Department of Motor Vehicles;

- A passport issued by the Department of State of the United States;

- A valid consular identification document issued by a consulate from the applicant's country of citizenship, or a valid passport from the applicant's country of citizenship; or

- An employee identification card issued by an agency or office of the State of California, or by an agency or office of a agency or office of a city, county, or city and county in this state.

Methods of Delivery of Notification:

The new law changes also expand the methods of delivering formal notices and communications to include any means of physical delivery that provides a receipt for official notices and requests for information from the Secretary of State to a notary public and communication and notices (e.g. changes of address) from a notary public to the Secretary of State.

Maximum Fees:

Government Code section 8211 and 8233 were amended to increase the maximum fees which may be charged for certain notarial acts. The new maximum fees are as follows:

Description	Maximum Fee
Acknowledgement or proof of a deed or other instrument, to include The seal and writing of the certificate	$15 for each signature
Administering an oath or affirmation to one person	$15

Executing the jurat including the seal	$15
All services rendered in connection with taking of any deposition	$30
Additional services rendered in connection with taking of any deposition • Administering the oath to the witness • Certificate to the deposition	$7 each
Notarize signatures on vote by mail ballot identification envelopes or other voting materials	$0
Certifying a copy of a power of attorney under Probate Code section 4307	$15
United States military veteran's application or claim for a pension, allotment, allowance, compensation, insurance, or any other veteran's benefit (Section 6107)	$0
A notary public qualified and bonded as an immigration consultant may enter data, provided by a client, on immigration forms provided by a federal or state agency	$15 per individual each set of forms

Chapter 1

How to Become a California State Notary

COURSE OF STUDY REQUIREMENT

An applicant for a notary public commission must satisfactorily complete a six-hour course of study that is approved by the California Secretary of State concerning the function and duties of a notary public. (Government Code section 8201(a)(3)). Also, an applicant for a notary public commission who (1) holds an active notary public commission and (2) has satisfactorily completed a six-hour notary public education course approved by the California Secretary of State must satisfactorily complete a three hour refresher course approved by the California Secretary of State prior to **reappointment** as a notary public. (Government Code section 8201(b)(2)).

IN ORDER TO BE ADMITTED TO THE EXAM YOU NEED THE FOLLOWING ITEMS:

- A completed application form. Applications can be obtained from the office of Cooperative Personnel Services (C.P.S.) Notary Public Examination Services – 191 Lathrop Way, Suite A – Sacramento, CA 95815 – (916) 263-3520 – www.cps.ca.gov/takeatest/notary

- Proof of Completion certificate with photograph attached.

- Proper government-issued identification such as;

- A California driver's license or state issued identification card.

- A U.S. passport.

- A passport issued by a foreign government that is validly stamped for entry into the United States by Immigration and Naturalization Service.

- A driver's license or identification card from another state.

- A Canadian or a Mexican driver's license.

- A U.S. military ID card.

- A check or money order made payable to the **California Secretary of State.** For new notaries and renewals the fee is $40.00 and to retake a failed test, the fee is $20.00.

- Two sharpened #2 black lead pencils (C.P.S will have pencils if you forget yours).

The above documents must be current *or have been issued*

FAST FACTS:

You will be notified within 15 business days whether you passed or failed the exam.

70% or better is a passing score.

within the last five years (if expired, but issued within the last 5 years they are still acceptable). These IDs must contain a description of the person presenting it, a photograph, a number assigned by the issuing agency and a signature.

Don't forget your ID

Within 15 business days of taking the exam you will be notified, whether you have passed or failed the exam. This same notice will include your test score. *70% or better is a passing score - you must answer at least 21 of the 30 questions correctly.* If you fail the exam, you may retake the exam again at a cost of $20.00, and only once per calendar month. If you pass the examination you will receive instructions on where to have your fingerprints taken as part of your background investigation.

Students can find the date of exams that are currently being processed at *www.sos.ca.gov/business/notary/processing-times/* **In addition to passing the state exam, notary public applicants must also pass a background check prior to being granted their commission. Information on completing your background check and obtaining your fingerprint check can be found at:** www.sos.ca.gov/business/notary/checklist/fingerprints/ you will receive:

1) **your notary commission**;

> 2) a **Certificate of Authorization** (which allows you to purchase a seal)
>
> 3) a **list of authorized seal manufacturers**.
>
> 4) Two oaths of office will be included in the notary public commission packet. If you are renewing your commission, your package will be sent to you about 30 days before your commission expires.

Within 30 days of the commencement date of the commission, the notary public must take the oath of office and file the oath and bond with the county clerk in the county where the notary's principal place of business is or will be located. If the notary chooses to take the oath of office before another notary public, the oath must be administered in the county where the new notary public's principal place of business is or will be located and where the oath and bond will be filed. In addition, a notary public must execute a bond in the amount of $15,000. The County Recorder is the one that actually records your bond. If you take your oath of office before a currently commissioned notary public, the law allows you to file your bond with the county clerk by certified mail.

If you fail to take and file your oath and bond within this **30-day**

FAST FACTS:

If you fail to take and file your oath and bond within a thirty day period, your commission becomes invalid.

period, your commission will become invalid. You will then need to re-apply for a new commission.

To obtain a notary seal, present or mail your Certificate of Authorization to an authorized seal manufacturer. You may start using your seal on or after your commission starting date, as long as you have taken your oath and filed your bond with the county clerk, and obtained a journal.

A $15,000 4 year bond cost approximately $38

QUALIFICATIONS FOR A CALIFORNIA NOTARY

To qualify to become a California notary, the applicant must be:

- A legal resident of the State of California

- At least 18 years of age.

In addition, the applicant must have:

- Satisfactorily completed a course of study approved by the Secretary of State (Government Code section 8201(a)(3) and 8201(b)(2)).

- Satisfactorily passed the written examination as prescribed by the Secretary of State. (Government Code section 8201(a)(4)).

- Pass a background check.

- Had no conviction or pending trial for a felony or lesser offense involving moral turpitude or of a nature incompatible with the duties of a notary. The Secretary of State may deny an application for the grounds stated. (Government Code section 8214.1)

- Persons who have not held a notary public commission in addition to those renewing their commissions, are required to have their fingerprints taken or re-taken at a live scan location, as directed by the secretary of state. All applicants must pass a background check along with fingerprinting. (Government Code 8201.1)

FAST FACTS:

U.S. Citizenship is not required, but California residency is required.

Prior to granting an appointment as a notary public, the Secretary of State shall determine that the applicant possesses the required honesty, credibility, truthfulness, and integrity to fulfill the responsibilities of the position. To assist in determining the identity of the applicant and whether the applicant has been convicted of a disqualifying crime specified in subdivision of Section 8214.1, the Secretary of State shall require that applicants be fingerprinted.

Applicants shall submit to the Department of Justice fingerprint images and related information required by the department for the purpose of obtaining information as to the existence and content of a record of state and federal convictions and arrests and information as to the existence and content of a record of state and federal arrests for which the department establishes that the person is free on bail, or on his or her recognizance, pending trial or appeal.(Government Code section 8201.1)

For more information about disqualifying crimes, please review the Notary Public Disciplinary Guidelines, available on the California Secretary of State's website at www.sos.ca.gov/notary/ (California Code of Regulations, title 2, section 20804).

As a notary public your term of office starts when you complete all of the prerequisites listed above and ends 4 years later. The exact start and end dates are listed on your actual commission certificate that you receive from the Secretary of State (Government Code section 8204).

OTHER CALIFORNIA NOTARY PUBLIC EDUCATION FACTS

- Jurisdiction is statewide (valid in all 58 counties).

- Length of term is four years. Term of office begins after you take, subscribe, and file your oath of office and file a $15,000 surety bond with the county clerk

- A notary public must execute a bond in the amount of $15,000. *(cost is about $38 for a four-year bond).* (Government Code sections 8212 through 8214).

- Errors and Omissions Insurance is not required, but it is highly recommended *(cost is about $51 for a four year, $15,000 policy*

- California notary law requires every notary to keep a journal of notarial acts. (Government Code section 8206).

- A notary seal is required. A self-inking rubber notary stamp is the *preferred* notary seal.

- The application fee and renewal fee are both $40.00 each and the test re-take fee is $20.00.

U.S. Citizenship is not required, but California legal residency is (no time requirement). Exception made for military personnel who must be U. S. citizens but state residency is not required. (Government Code section 8201)

A notary public shall not use a commercial mail receiving agency

FAST FACTS:

The law requires you to notify the Secretary of State, by certified mail, of any status changes such as a change of your principal place of business or residence within 30 days.

or post office box as his or her principal place of business or residence, unless the notary public also provides the Secretary of State with a physical street address as the principal place of residence. Willful failure to notify the Secretary of State of a change of address shall be punishable as an infraction by a fine of not more than five hundred dollars ($500).(Government Code 8213.5).

A notary public must notify the Secretary of State in writing by certified mail within 30 days of any changes in their business or residential address, (Government Code section 8213.5). To insure the proper processing of your notice, send a copy of your commission certificate or include your name exactly as it appears on your commission, along with your expiration date and commission number.

If you leave office for any reason, or allow your appointment to expire <u>for</u> more than 30 days, all-notarial records and papers must be delivered within 30 days, to the clerk of the county in which your oath is on file. Failure to do so is a misdemeanor, and you will be personally liable for damages to any person injured by that action or inaction. If you leave office, your seal should be destroyed.

If a notary public transfers the principal place of business from one county to another, the notary public **may** file a new oath of office and bond or a duplicate of the original bond with the county clerk to which the principal place of business was transferred. Keep in mind that the law requires you to notify the secretary of state of your status change. <u>However, there is no requirement to re-file in your new county.</u> If the notary public elects to make a new filing, the notary public shall, within 30 days of the filing, obtain an official seal, which shall include the name of the county to which the notary public has transferred. In the case where the notary public elects to make a new filing, the same filing and recording fees are applicable as in the case of the original filing and recording of the bond. (Government Code sections 8213 and 8213.5).

FAST FACTS:

The main purpose of a notary is to assist in the prevention of fraud.

If a notary public submits an application to change his or her name to the Secretary of State, the notary public shall, within 30 days from the date an amended commission is issued, file a new oath of office and an amendment to the bond with the county clerk in which the principal place of business is located. The amended commission with the name change shall not take effect unless the filing is completed within the 30-day period. The amended commission with the name change takes effect the date the oath and amendment to the bond is filed with the county clerk. If the principal place of business address was changed in the application for name change, either a new or duplicate of the original bond shall be filed with the county clerk with the amendment to the bond. The notary public shall, within 30 days of the filing, obtain an official seal that includes the name of the notary public and the name of the county to which the notary public has transferred, if applicable.

The recording fee specified in (Government Code section 27361) shall be paid by the person appointed a notary public. The fee may be paid to the county clerk who shall transmit it to the county recorder.

The county recorder shall record the bond and shall thereafter mail, unless specified to the contrary, it to the person named in the instrument and, if no person is named, to the party leaving it for recording.

The **California Secretary of State** is the chief elections officer of the state. The Secretary of State's responsibles include:

- Serving as the state's Chief Elections Officer

- Implementing electronic filing and Internet disclosure of campaign and lobbyist financial information

- Maintaining business filings

- Commissioning notaries public

- Operating the Safe at Home Confidential Address Program

- Maintaining the Domestic Partners and Advance Health Care Directive Registries

- Safeguarding the State Archives

- Serving as a trustee of the California Museum for History, Women & the Arts

The Secretary of State is elected to four-year terms, concurrent with the other constitutional officers of California, and is restricted by term limits to only two terms. The Secretary of State may appoint and commission notaries public in such number, as the Secretary of State deems necessary for the public convenience.

FAST FACTS:

A notary's main pupose is to detect and deter fraud.

Office of the Secretary of State
Phone: (916) 653-3595
Notary Public section
Mailing address: PO Box 942877
Sacramento, CA 94277-0001
www.sos.ca.gov/notary/
Street Address: 1500 - 11th St., Second Floor
Sacramento, CA 95814

THREE COMPONENTS OF A NOTARY PUBLIC

There are 3 main components of a notary public. First he or she must be a person of proven integrity, a state officer, and an impartial or neutral witness to a particular transaction. (Government Code section 8201.1).

1) Proven Integrity

Since a notary's main purpose is to detect and deter fraud, California's statutes require notaries to be of "good moral character." If a person has been convicted of embezzlement or fraud, he or she is not considered to be of "good moral character." As an example, a non-felony traffic violation, such as a speeding ticket, isn't relevant to notarial functions and wouldn't disqualify you from obtaining a notarial commission.

2) Ministerial Officer of the State

A notary public is commissioned by The Secretary of State and acts as an officer of the state. Since the office is ministerial rather than regulatory or judicial, the duties of a notary are narrowly defined to certain prescribed acts of limited scope. A notary must follow written rules that allow only limited discretion in performing these acts. Notaries are expected to have and exercise good common sense.

3) Impartial Witness

Another important function of a notary is to be impartial. Impartial means:

The notary is not named in the document and he or she has no financial or beneficial interest in the transaction. A notary simply witnesses the signing of a document and takes acknowledgements as a neutral or impartial party to the transaction. In other words, the notary has nothing to gain by notarizing the document beyond his notarization fee.

FAST FACTS:

Employers need to know that you are an officer of the state as well as their employee.

Notary

WHAT IS A NOTARY?

A responsible person appointed by the Secretary of State to witness or verify the signing of important documents and administer oaths. <u>Notaries are technically ministerial officials.</u> (Government Code Section 8205)

The Secretary of State may refuse to appoint any person as a notary public or fine, suspend, or revoke the commission of any notary public if the Secretary finds that there has been a violation of Government Code section 8214.1.

Should the Secretary of State determine that a notary public has committed a punishable act, the notary public's resignation or lapse in commission does not bar the Secretary from initiating or continuing an investigation. Additionally, upon completion of the investigation the Secretary maintains authority to institute disciplinary action. (California Code section 8214.4)

Keep in mind prior to a revocation or suspension or after a denial of a commission, or prior to the imposition of a civil penalty, the person affected shall have a right to a hearing on the matter and the proceeding shall be conducted in accordance with Chapter 5 (commencing with Section 11500) of Part 1 of Division 3, except that a person shall not have a right to a hearing after a denial of an application for a notary public commission in either of the following cases: (Government Code section 8214.3).

(a) The Secretary of State has, within one year previous to the application, and after proceedings conducted in accordance with Chapter 5 (commencing with Section 11500) of Part 1 of Division 3, denied or revoked the applicant's application or commission.

(b) The Secretary of State has entered an order pursuant to Section 8214.4 finding that the applicant has committed or omitted acts constituting grounds for suspension or revocation of a notary public's commission (Government Code section 8214.3).

Should you be convicted of a crime related to notarial misconduct (including the false completion of a notarial certificate) or any felony, the court must revoke your commission and require you to surrender your notary seal to the court to be forwarded to the Secretary of State along with a certified copy of the judgment of conviction (Government Code section 8214.8).

Sign Here:

X_____

FAST FACTS:

We need notaries to prove the authenticity of the signature

The actions or inactions that are punishable by civil penalty that may not exceed one thousand five hundred dollars (($1,500) for a violation of Government Code section 8214.1 subdivisions.

(f) The use of false or misleading advertising wherein the notary public has represented that the notary public has duties, rights, or privileges that he or she does not possess by law.

(i) Commission of any act involving dishonesty, fraud, or deceit with the intent to substantially benefit the notary public or another, or substantially injure another.

(l) Execution of any certificate as a notary public containing any statement known to the notary public to be false.

(m) No notary public who holds himself or herself out as being an immigration specialist, immigration consultant or any other title or description reflecting an expertise in immigration matters shall advertise in any manner whatsoever that he or she is a notary public.

(p) Every notary public who is not an attorney who advertises the services of a notary public in a language other than English by signs or other means of written communication, with the exception of a single desk plaque, shall post with that advertisement a notice in English and in the other language which sets forth the following this statement: *"I am not an attorney and, therefore, cannot give legal advice about immigration or any other legal matters."*

The maximum fees are set by statute which a notary public may charge.

The notice required by subdivision; (a) shall be printed and posted as prescribed by the Secretary of State.

Literal translation of the phrase "notary public" into Spanish, hereby defined as "notario publico" or "notario," is prohibited. For purposes of this subdivision, "literal translation" of a word or phrase from one language to another means the translation of a word or phrase without regard to the true meaning of the word or phrase in the language which is being translated. (Government Code sections 8219.5(c) and 8223 (a),

The Secretary of State shall suspend for a period of not less than one year or revoke the commission of any notary public

FAST FACTS:

Notary fees must not be more than those established by California statute.

who fails to comply with subdivision (a) or (c). However, on the second offense the commission of such notary public shall be revoked permanently in addition to any commissioning or disciplinary sanctions. (Government Code section 8214.1).

The actions or inactions that are punishable by civil penalties that may or may not exceed seven hundred fifty dollars ($750) for a violation of Government Code section 8214.1 subdivisions.

(h) Charging more than the fees prescribed in Government Code section 8211.

(j) Failure to complete the acknowledgment at the time the notary's signature and seal are affixed to the document.

(k) Failure to administer the oath or affirmation as required by paragraph (3) of subdivision (a) of Section 8205.

(d) Failure to discharge fully and faithfully any of the duties or responsibilities required of a notary public, (Government Code section 8214.1 and 8214.15).

WHY DO WE NEED NOTARIES?

- To assist in the prevention of fraud. (This is the main purpose of a notary).
- To prove the authenticity of the signature.
- To administer oaths to compel truthfulness.

MAY ANY SIGNATURE BE NOTARIZED?

- To notarize you must have text committing the signer.
- To notarize you must have an original signature.
- To notarize you must issue a notarial certificate.

THREE PARTS TO ANY NOTARIZATION

- Identifying the constituents or administering the oath.
- Making a record in the notarial journal.
- Filling out a notarial certificate.

CALIFORNIA NOTARIES PERFORM THE FOLLOWING SERVICES (Government Code Section 8205*):

- Acknowledgments
- Jurats

FAST FACTS:

A written agreement between you and your employer regarding notary fees is advisable.

- Copy Certifications

    1. Notarial records

    2. Powers of Attorney

- Protests

PRIVATE EMPLOYERS AND NOTARIES

It is important to discuss notary requirements and other issues with your employer ahead of time. Employers need to know that you are an officer of the state as well as their employee and that cooperation is the best way of getting what everyone wants: valid notarizations done efficiently.

RESPONSIBILITIES OF EMPLOYERS AND NOTARIES

A notary has an ethical obligation to serve as a notary public. Notaries exist not for the convenience of a business, but to serve the common good. The general public (private individuals) also needs to have access to the services of a notary.

At the same time, under California law, employers may prohibit notaries from notarizing documents for non-customers during regular work hours. For example, a title company, at their discretion, may only allow its notaries (escrow officers) to notarize documents involving currently-opened escrows during regular work hours. (Government Code 8202.7 and 8202.8)

EMPLOYERS MAY NOT PROHIBIT NOTARIES FROM NOTARIZING ON THEIR OWN TIME.

Employers may not limit or restrict an employee/notary from notarizing documents on their own time. An employer may only limit a notary's activities during the employee's ordinary course of employment.

It should be clear that employers may prohibit notaries from notarizing documents for non-customers during the ordinary course of business only if an agreement exists pursuant to Government Code subsection 8202.7 (Government Code subsection 8202.8). Further, notaries should understand that a prohibition may apply to transactions that are not directly associated with business purposes of the employer, rather than to "non-customers." The agreement referenced in Government Code subsection 8202.7 could provide for the remission of notary fees to the employer even if notarizations occurred outside of the employee's ordinary course of business.

If your employer insists that you notarize a document in a

FAST FACTS:

The Notary Public Institute recommends that notaries public establish and post, in a conspicuous place, the days and times that they are available to notarize documents.

manner inconsistent with California laws and rules, you and the employer should be aware of laws regarding notaries who are forced to break the law, or "commit misconduct." For example, if your employer asks you to notarize an acknowledgment without the signing party present, that action would be intentional misconduct and would subject you to a fine, a suspension, or revoking of your commission.

EMPLOYER NOTARIZATION POLICIES

Companies that employ notaries might want to create a policy on notarization. Such a policy should address the following issues:

What times a notary will be available? The Notary Public Institute recommends that all notaries public post a conspicuous sign, at their place of business, showing the days and times that they are available to the public to notarize documents. You are expected to serve the public during the times that you have established as your hours of operation. <u>The law does not require notaries public to be available during any set time period.</u>

What types of documents will be permitted. For example, a hospital might allow notarization of only healthcare documents. Although an Attorney General's opinion (DOJ 165-300-0093) states, "...the notary public may, under the notaries public laws, either serve the entire public which desires notary services, a portion of the public (such as customers of a business or fellow employees) or no one at all.

NOTARY FEES AND YOUR PRIVATE EMPLOYER

A private employer, pursuant to an agreement with an employee who is a notary public, may pay the premiums on any bond and the cost of any stamps, seals, or other supplies required in connection with the appointment, commission, or performance of the duties of such notary public.

Notwithstanding any other provision of law, a private employer of a notary public who has entered into an agreement with his or her employee pursuant to Government Code section 8202.7 may limit, during the employee's ordinary course of employment, the providing of notarial services by the employee solely to transactions directly associated with the business purposes of the employer.

California statutes and rules address the collection of notary fees by employers, but a written agreement about notary fees is advisable. The statute gives only the notary public the right to

FAST FACTS:

A notary public has an ethical obligation to serve the public.

charge notary fees, but an employer often includes a notary charge to the constituent when notarization takes place. All fees collected by the employer or the notary should be placed into a fund from which the salary of the notary public is paid. (Government Code sections 6100, 8202.5, 8202.7 and 8202.8) The fees must not be more than those established by Government Code section 8211. The agreement should make it clear that the notary gives the employer the right to collect and retain the appropriate revenue on his or her behalf. The employer should draw up an appropriate agreement between him or herself and the notary.

Notaries who charge for their service will find the maximum fees allowed to be charged in Government Code section 8211. The notary public may charge up to the maximum fees listed, but must not charge more, to do so could result in a fine, suspension, or revocation of the notary's commission. The notary public must keep track of all fees collected by making an entry in his or her notarial journal (Government Code section 8211). Please see maximum allowable fee schedule in Chapter 5.

NOTARY FEES AND YOUR PUBLIC EMPLOYER

Additionally, upon written notice, the notary public must furnish the Secretary of State, within the time specified by the Secretary of State, certified copies of the notary public's journal. (Government Code section 8205(b)(1)). The second duty is the notary public must respond within 30 days of receiving a written request sent by certified mail from the Secretary of State's office for information relating to official acts performed as a notary public. (Government Code section 8205(b)(2)).

A notary public may also use the following declaration on copies of the journal copies. "I hereby certify that this is a true and correct copy of my original notary public journal in my possession." The notary public must sign his/her name and affix the notary stamp below the statement. (Government Code section 8205 and 8206)

Officers of the state, or of a county or judicial district, shall not perform any official services unless upon the payment of the fees prescribed by law for the performance of the services. This shall not be construed to prohibit any notary public, except a notary public whose fees are required by law, from performing notarial services without charging a fee.

The Secretary of State may appoint and commission the number

FAST FACTS:

Notaries who charge for their service will find the maximum fees allowed to be charged in Government Code section 8211.

of state, city, county, and public school district employees as notaries public to act for and on behalf of the governmental entity for which appointed which the Secretary of State deems proper. Whenever a notary is appointed and commissioned, a duly authorized representative of the employing governmental entity shall execute a certificate that the appointment is made for the purposes of the employing governmental entity, and whenever the certificate is filed with any state or county officer, no fees shall be charged by the officer for the filing or issuance of any document in connection with the appointment.

The state or any city, county, or school district for which the notary public is appointed and commissioned pursuant to this section may pay from any funds available for its support the premiums on any bond and the cost of any stamps, seals, or other supplies required in connection with the appointment, commission, or performance of the duties of the notary public. Any fees collected or obtained by any notary public whose documents have been filed without charge and for whom bond premiums have been paid by the employer of the notary public shall be remitted by the notary public to the employing agency which shall deposit the funds to the credit of the fund from which the salary of the notary public is paid.

FAST FACTS:

The main purpose of a notary is to establish the identity of an individual and assist in the prevention of fraud

Chapter 1

TEST YOUR KNOWLEDGE

1) California notaries receive their commission from the Secretary of State.
   a) True
   b) False

2) California notaries can notarize documents anywhere in the State.
   a) True
   b) False

3) Notaries are classified as ministerial officials
   a) True
   b) False

4) Anyone wishing to become a California State notary must be at least 18 years of age.
   a) True
   b) False

5) Anyone wishing to become a California State notary must be a US citizen.
   a) True
   b) False

6) Anyone wishing to become a California State notary must be a legal resident of the State of California.

   a) True
   b) False

7) California notaries are required to file a bond of $15,000.00 with the County Clerk's office within 30 calendar days of their commission date.
   a) True
   b) False

8) California's Secretary of State's term of office is four years.
   a) True
   b) False

9) A notary must notify the Secretary of State within 30 calendar days, in writing via Certified Mail if their business or residential address changes.
   a) True
   b) False

10) California notaries are required to maintain Errors and Omissions Insurance.
    a) True
    b) False

Chapter 2

Misconduct

A notary public is responsible for knowing and understanding California laws and administrative rules relating to notaries. They can be found in Government Code (Chapter 3, Division 1, Title 2), Civil Code, Code of Civil Procedure, Business and Professions Code, Elections Code, and Uniform Commercial Code (U.U.C.). Your actions as a notary are governed by these sets of laws.

Notaries must also be aware that every person who, with the intent to defraud, knowing that he or she has no authority to do so, counterfeits or forges the seal or handwriting of another person or of a fictitious person may be guilty of forgery. This includes a person who falsifies the acknowledgment of a notary public (Penal Code section 470(d), 473 and Government Code section 6203).

Additionally, a notary public may be guilty of forgery (which is a felony or a misdemeanor), if he or she makes or gives any certificate, writing or statement and delivers it as true which he or she knows to be false. Every officer authorized by law to make or give any certificate or other writing is guilty of a felony or a misdemeanor if he or she makes and delivers as true any certificate or writing containing statements which he or she knows to be false or is guilty of a felony punishable by a term of imprisonment in a county jail for 16 months, or two or three years.

Prosecution for a violation of this offense shall be commenced within four years after discovery of the commission of the offense, or within four years after the completion of the offense, whichever is later. The penalty provided by this section is not an exclusive remedy, and does not affect any other relief or remedy provided by law (Government Code subsection 6203 and Penal Code section 470(d)).

[Forgery is punishable by imprisonment in the state prison, or by imprisonment in county jail for not more than one year or by imprisionment to subdivision (h) of section 1170 (Penal Code section 473)]

The Secretary of State's office staff is available to assist you if you are having any trouble understanding your obligations with respect to notary law. It is up to the notary to make sure that he or she understands their obligation and requirements under the law.

FAST FACTS:

Unintentional misconduct is negligent behavior that causes a notary to make an error in a notarization or to accidently forget to do what is required.

CONFLICT OF INTEREST

Conflict of interest is defined as any situation in which a notary is in a position to exploit his or her official capacity in some way for personal gain. "A notary public who has a direct financial or beneficial interest in a transaction shall not perform any notorial act in connection with such transaction." If the notary is named in the document to be notarized whether receiving direct benefit or not you are not eligible to notarize these documents.

A notary public is not prohibited from notarizing for relatives or others, unless doing so would provide a direct financial or beneficial interest to the notary public. With California's community property law, care should be exercised if notarizing for a spouse or a domestic partner.

FINANCIAL OR BENEFICIAL INTEREST

A direct financial or beneficial interest in a transaction if the notary public:

(a) With respect to a financial transaction, is named, individually, as a principal to the transaction.

(b) With respect to real property, is named, individually, as agrantor, grantee, mortgagor, mortgagee, trustor, trustee,beneficiary, vendor, vendee, lessor, or lessee, to the transaction.

A notary public has no direct financial or beneficial interest in a transaction where the notary public acts in the capacity of an agent, employee, insurer, attorney, escrow, or lender for a person having a direct financial or beneficial interest in the transaction. (Government Code section 8224).

AVOIDING MISCONDUCT

Negligent or purposeful improper notarization is called "misconduct." Misconduct can be either **intentional** or **unintentional.**

Intentional misconduct is deliberate disobedience of notarial statute, rule, or good practice that seeks to benefit the notary in some way, often to defraud the signer of the document.

For example, a notary would be unable to notarize a grant deed that transferred property to him or herself because they would be named in the document and would receive direct financial and beneficial gain from this transaction.

Unintentional misconduct is negligent behavior that causes a notary to make an error in a notarization or to accidentally forget to do what is required. For example, failure to supply the name of

FAST FACTS:

Civil penalties are the penalties notaries public are most afraid of incurring.

the county in the venue portion of a notarial certificate could be an omission that is deemed unintentional misconduct.

Most misconduct is the result of disobeying the law, whether the notary gives help beyond what the law allows, or fails to do everything the law requires.

Notaries public must not give legal advice. Do not tell people which legal procedure to do, how to do it, or what they need to do to get a legal action accomplished. You may think you know what to do, but you open yourself up to a lawsuit even if you are right. The California State Bar takes a dim view of unlicensed individuals giving out legal advice. This even applies to notarial certificates. As you'll see, a notary may not suggest or select notarial certificates for people. Rather, he or she performs a particular notarization at the direction of the requesting individual.

Notaries public must not prepare documents. Don't fill out documents or finish drafting them, even as a favor. It takes an attorney to know what is legally appropriate for a document.

Finally, notaries public must be very careful as they perform their notary duties not to accidentally unlawfully practice law (by giving legal advice or completing legal documents for their constituents). Any person … practicing law who is not an active member of the State Bar, or otherwise authorized pursuant to statue or court rule to practice law in this state at the time doing so, is guilty of a misdemeanor punishable by up to one year in a county jail or by a fine up to one thousand dollars ($1,000.00), or both (Business and Professions Code section 6126).

COMMON EXAMPLES OF NOTIORIAL MISCONDUCT

- Didn't make signer appear before the notary.

- Didn't properly identify the signer.

- Didn't lock up the notary seal and journal so that others couldn't use them.

- Didn't keep a notarial journal.

UNLIMITED LIABILITY

Because so many documents and judgments based on those documents rely on the validity of the notarization, breaches of notarial law are taken very seriously. There are three kinds of penalties that notaries can incur through their misconduct: **administrative**, **criminal**, and **civil**.

Administrative penalties are levied by the Secretary of State, and can range from an advice letter to revocation of the commission and or a fine. It is important to avoid such penalties

FAST FACTS:

There are three kinds of penalties a notary can incur, (1) administrative (2) criminal, and (3) civil

because they may have other consequences. For example, many licensing agencies will not issue a license if a notary commission has been revoked or suspended.

Criminal penalties are given in cases of fraud, coercion, or other criminal action. In these cases, the notary has intentionally committed misconduct and is prosecuted in the same way as for any crime.

Civil penalties are the penalties notaries public are most afraid of incurring. If a notary, through carelessness or inaction, unintentionally or intentionally damages the complainant, he or she is liable for monetary damages without limit. For example, if an improperly notarized grant deed causes the deal to fall through, and that action or inaction costs the signer thousands of dollars, the notary can be sued so that the signer recovers those losses.

A notarization is not just a "formality," but it must be done with due diligence and care. This liability is neither new nor unusual, and notaries should not be unduly alarmed. However, it underscores the serious nature of notarization and the importance of developing competence and understanding in the performance of notarial duties.

A notary public must exercise great care when notarizing deeds that affect real property. Any notary that knowingly and willfully with the intent to commit fraud in the notarization of a deed of trust on real property, consisting of a single-family residence through a four unit dwelling, with knowledge that the deed of trust contains any false statements or is forged in whole or in part, is guilty of a felony (Government Code section 8214.2).

Every person who files any false or forged document or instrument with the county recorder which affects title to, places an encumbrance on, or places an interest secured by a mortgage or deed of trust on real property consisting of a single-family residence containing not more than four dwelling units, with knowledge that the document is false or forged, is punishable, in addition to any other punishment, by a fine not to exceed seventy-five thousand dollars ($75,000.00). Additionally, every person who makes a sworn statement to a notary public, with knowledge that the statement is false, to induce the notary public to perform an improper notarial act on an instrument or document affecting title to, or placing an encumbrance on real property consisting of a single-family residence containing not more than four dwelling units is guilty of a felony (Penal Code 115.5).

Notary law further states that any person who solicits, coerces, or

FAST FACTS:

Describe your notarial act, and especially anything odd or unusual in your journal.

in any manner influences a notary public to perform an improper notarial act, including any act required of a notary public under Government Code section 8206, with the knowledge that the act is an improper notarial act is guilty of a misdemeanor (Government Code section 8225).

The penalty provided by Government Code section 8225 is not an exclusive remedy, and does not effect any other relief of remedy provided by law. Violations of this section include but are not limited to: coercing or influencing a notary public to complete a false certificate of acknowledgment or jurat; (2) coercing or influencing a notary public to not enter required information in the official journal or; (3) coercing or influencing a notary public to input false information in the official journal or; (4) coercing or influencing a notary public to falsely modify a journal entry.

If any person knowingly destroys, defaces, or conceals any records or papers belonging to the office of a notary public that person is guilty of a misdemeanor and is liable in civil action for damages to any person injured as a result of such destruction, defacing, or concealment (Government Code section 8221).

It is a misdemeanor for any person to; (1) represent or hold himself or herself out to be a notary public or to give any person the impression that they are entitled to act as a notary public, (2) assume , use or advertise the title of notary public in such a way as to convey the impression that they are a notary public or (3) purport to act as a notary public unless they are duly commissioned, qualified, and acting as a notary for the State of California (Government Code section 8227.1).

REASONABLE CARE

Reasonable care is "that degree of care which a person of ordinary prudence would exercise in the same or similar circumstances." Although California law does not specifically state this, the standard notaries public must adhere to is *reasonable care*. Reasonable care is "that degree of care which a person of ordinary prudence would exercise in the same or similar circumstances," according to Black's Law Dictionary. If a notary acts with reasonable care when performing a notarization, the courts have always held that the notary acted with sufficient diligence and is not subject to damages.

PERJURY

Every person who, having taken an oath that he or she will

FAST FACTS:

Mistakes do happen.... Any corrections must be noted in your journal. If you accidently put the wrong date on a certificate or misspell a word you can correct the error before the constituent leaves with the document.

testify, declare, depose, or certify truly before any competent tribunal, officer, or person, in any of the cases in which the oath may by law of the State of California be administered, willfully and contrary to the oath, states as true any material matter which he or she knows to be false, and every person who testifies, declares, deposes, or certifies under penalty of perjury in any of the cases in which the testimony, declarations, depositions, or certification is permitted by law of the State of California under penalty of perjury and willfully states as true any material matter which he or she knows to be false is guilty of perjury (Penal Code 118).

OBEY ALL LAWS AND REGULATIONS

The most important thing to remember about reasonable care is that you are required to know and understand what the law requires of you. In other words: Do what the law says you should do and don't do what it says you shouldn't do. Always use Good Judgment and Common Sense.

Many of the situations that the notary public encounters are not precisely spelled out in law. The law gives general guidelines but relies on the notary's common sense to properly evaluate each situation. For example, notaries may use a driver's license to identify a signer, but if the ID looks false (a tampered photo, an obviously incorrect birth date, sex, or height, etc.), then the notary has a duty to act appropriately. Although many of the instructions in this guide have no direct counterpart in statute, they are good common sense practices that will help the notary avoid any appearance of wrongdoing or insufficient care.

See the signer √ It's important that the signer personally appears before you for every single notarization. Remember, the document signer must sign your journal, as well as provide specific information and be readily identified. Besides, it's the law.

Obey the law √ Even if your employer paid for your commission and supplies, the commission is your responsibility and you are accountable. A notary public is responsible to uphold the laws of the state, and employer policies or directions that violate that law should not be followed. Know what the law requires and forbids, and follow it.

Lock-up the journal & seal √ The notary journal is your best protection and the only record of the notarization; it is crucial that it remain safe. Likewise, the seal, which uniquely identifies you to anyone examining your notarization, must be accessible only to you. (Government Code section 8206(a)) Otherwise, neither journal nor seal are reliable, and therefore suspect in court.

FAST FACTS:

Notaries can only certify copies of the Notary's own "Official Records" and "Powers of Attorney."

(Government Codes section 8207 and 8228).

Identify the signer by requiring proper identification. Anyone who reads the notary certificate trusts that the signer did indeed sign and is the party stated in the document, and it is absolutely imperative that the notary make sure of that. In identifying:

If the signer is identified by satisfactory evidence he or she must provide you with a primary piece of identification. If using a credible witness the notary must know the credible witness and the credible witness must swear to the identity of the principal. If using a subscribing witness the law also requires a party signing any document affecting real property to place his or her thumbprint in the notary public's journal. This does not apply to a trustee's deed resulting from a decree of foreclosure or a non-judicial foreclosure pursuant to Civil Code section 2924, or to a deed of re-conveyance.

Get good identification from the signer, always look for signs of alterations or signs of fraud. Describe (in detail) the notarial act in the journal, this is probably the most important thing you can do to protect yourself and others. So, please describe your notarial act, and especially anything odd or unusual, in your journal.

Haste makes waste! You may encounter a constituent impatiently waiting to get through the "red tape" of notarizing a document. It is important to remain calm and make sure you notarize correctly or you may later wish you had been more careful.

Sometimes a constituent or employer may insist that you do something contrary to notary law. It's important to stand your ground and remind your boss (in a less stressful moment) that it's important to both of you that the notarization is properly done.

FAST FACTS:

It is especially important to avoid administrative penalties because they may have additional consequences.

Following are detailed steps for correctly notarizing a document. The steps should be followed in order to ensure that you get the information you need before the notarization process is complete and the client has left.

THE PROCESS

1) Screen the signer (constituent) and the document

- Require personal appearance

- Make a careful identification

- Scan the document for information and verify its completeness

2) Jot the information in your journal

- Check the document date

- Compare the signer's signature on the document against the name on the ID

- Complete the journal entries

3) Complete the constituent's certificate

- Complete the Certificate that you were asked to complete

- Certificate must fit the notarization

- Affix notary seal and signature

- If using loose leaf certificates staple them to the left margin of the document

MAKING CORRECTIONS

Mistakes do happen. The notary may accidentally put the wrong date on the certificate. The signer's name may be misspelled on the certificate. All of these things can be corrected. The Notary Public Institute recommends that the notary make notes in his or her journal of any corrections that were made.

CORRECTING DURING THE NOTARIZATION

Don't use whiteout.
Line through incorrect information in ink, print the correct information immediately above and initial and date nearby.
Reapply seal if it has been smeared.

CORRECTING AFTER THE NOTARIZATION

Never allow anyone else to change your certificate. It is your responsibility to correct errors and omissions on the certificates you complete before the constituient leaves.

Never send a completed certificate for someone else to attach. The document must be brought to you and you must attach the certificate.

COPY CERTIFICATIONS

California law authorizes notaries public to only certify copies of the **notary's own official records and power of attorney**. Persons requesting certified copies of documents other than these two types should be referred to the official who has custody of the original document or to the place or office where the document has been officially filed or recorded. (Government Code sections 8205(a)(4)), 8205(b)(1) and 8206 (e) (subpoena or court order) and Probate Code section 4307).

Additionally, upon written notice, the notary public must furnish the Secretary of State, within the time specified by the Secretary of

FAST FACTS:

Always use good judgement and common sense as you carry out your duties as a notary public.

State, certified copies of the notary public's journal. (Government Code section 8205(b)(1)). The second duty is the notary public must respond within 30 days of receiving a written request sent by certified mail from the Secretary of State's office for information relating to official acts performed as a notary public. (Government Code section 8205(b)(2)).

* **Notary certificate for certified copy of a journal:**

State of   (___California___)ss

County of   (_____)

On this _____ day of _____, ____,

I,_____(_name of notary_)_____, the undersigned notary public, hereby declare that the attached reproduction of a notary journal entry involving _____(_describe document - noting date and signers)_____ is a true, and correct photocopy made from a page in my notary journal.

Witness my hand and official seal.

_____

Notary's Signature   Seal

A notary public may also use the following declaration on copies of the journal copies. _"I hereby certify that this is a true and correct copy of my original notary public journal in my possession."_ The notary public must sign his/her name and affix the notary stamp below the statement. (Government Code section 8205 and 8206)

* **Notary certificate for a certified copy of an <u>original</u> power of attorney:**

State of   (___California___)ss

County of   (_____)

I,_____(_name of notary_)_____, Notary Public certify that

On this _____ day of _____, ____,

FAST FACTS:

A notarization is not just a formality; it must be done with due care and diligence.

I examined the original power of attorney and the copy of the power of attorney. I further certify that the copy is a true and correct copy of the original power of attorney.

Witness my hand and official seal.

_____

Notary's Signature   Seal

There are civil penalties that a notary public may be subject to for his or her action or inaction. These civil penalties include fines not to exceed fifteen hundred dollars ($1,500.00) if the disciplinary sanction is a violation of subdivision (f), (i), (l), (m) or (p) of section 8214.1. Additionally, there are civil penalties that include fines not to exceed seven hundred and fifty dollars ($750.00) if the disciplinary sanction is in violation of subdivision (h), (j), or (k) and subdivision (d) if the violation is a negligent violation (Government Code section 8214.15).

FAST FACTS:

Never send a completed certificate for someone else to attach. The document must be brought to you and you must attach the certificate.

Chapter 2

TEST YOUR KNOWLEDGE

1) A notary is responsible for knowing and understanding California notary laws and administrative rules relating to notaries.

    a) True
    b) False

2) Negligent or purposed improper notarization is called misconduct.

    a) True
    b) False

3) Notaries are liable for both intentional and unintentional misconduct.
    a) True
    b) False

4) Notaries can never be held liable for criminal penalties.
    a) True
    b) False

5) In an emergency, a notary may notarize a document without the signer personally appearing.
    a) True
    b) False

6) When a notary chooses not to renew his or her commission the journal may be kept until their commission expires.
    a) True
    b) False

7) After receiving their commission, a notary has 30 days to file his or her bond and take the oath of office.
    a) True
    b) False

8) The notary's journal must be surrendered to the employer upon resignation of the notary/employee.
    a) True
    b) False

9) Regardless of the notary's intentions, a notary is liable for all damages sustained due to official misconduct.
    a) True
    b) False

10) Knowingly completing a false certification is a criminal violation.
    a) True
    b) False

Chapter 3

COMPLETING A NOTARY CERTIFICATE

It is your direct responsibility as a Notary Public to always practice reasonable care by:

- Exercising common sense.
- Obeying all the Notary laws and **never engaging in the unauthorized practice of law by preparing documents, giving legal advice or choosing notarial wording for the signer.**

Remember a Notary Public may not refuse to perform a notarial act based on a principal's race, age, gender, sexual orientation, religion, national origin, health or disability. Private notaries are not required to notarize non-clients or non customers of the Notary public's employer during regular business hours.

Before completing any notarization it is imperative that the signer and the Notary Public are physically together so that they can communicate with each other and present identification documents to the notary for review and verification. Never notarize a signature of a person who is not in your PRESENCE at the time of the notarization.

As a notary public you must be able to effectively communicate with the person requesting services. If an individual does not speak a language that you understand you should refer the individual to someone that understands and speaks his or her language. Notarizing documents that are in a language that you don't understand is acceptable as long as you can effectively communicate with the person requesting service. Using an interpreter is not an acceptable practice (Government Code section 8205).

A notary public can be subject to a civil penalty up to $10,000 for willfully stating as true any material fact that he or she knows to be false. In addition, a notary public may be guilty of forgery if he or she issues an acknowledgment knowing it to be false which may be a felony. (Civil Code section 1189, Penal Code section 470(d))

HOW TO PERFORM A NOTARIZATION STEP BY STEP

First - Identify the Signer (Person Requesting Notary)

Ask the person requesting your notary services for identification. Identification of a person should be based on one current document issued by a government agency (must be current or have been issued within the last 5 years if expired) bearing the photographic image of the person's face and signature, a serial or other identifying number and a physical description of the person, though a properly stamped passport without a physical description

FAST FACTS:

The jurat certificate must be attached to all affidavits subscribed and sworn to before a notary public.

is acceptable. In addition, one or two credible witnesses can be used as identification. (Civil Code section 1185)

Second - In an effort to help prevent fraud, The Notary Public Institute recommends that you verify that the signer understands the document.

You are not responsible for the contents of the document, however you should be satisfied that there is no compelling doubt about whether the signer is aware of what he/she is signing. The Notary Public Institute highly recommends that you establish the signer's willingness and competence. we further recommend that a notary public not notarize a document if the notary suspects that the signer is not acting on his/her own free will or is being coerced.

Third - Check the Document

Visually scan the entire document for completion before notarizing.

Fourth - Examine the Notorial Certificate

If notarial wording is not provided or indicated for a document, a non-attorney notary shall not determine the type of notarial act or certificate to be used; a non-attorney notary shall not assist another person in selecting, or understanding a document or transaction requiring a notarial act.   Most notarial certificates are preprinted and are already on the document(s):

(A) Note the venue: State of California

     County of _____

This language should reflect where the notarization is taking place.

(B) Check the date, and make sure it is the date that you are performing the notarization. A notary should never predate or postdate a notarial certificate.

(C) Identify whether you are administering a jurat (signer takes an oath or affirmation from the notary public) or acknowledgment (signer appears in person before the notary public and presents a document), copy certification or any other type of notarial act. You may refuse to notarize a document when the document does not have notarial language. You may suggest to the signer that he return the document to the issuing agency, the receiving agency or the individual that indicated it was necessary and ask that the proper notarial certificate be placed on the document, so that it may be notarized. Make sure that all the information required on the notarial certificate is completed.

FAST FACTS:

An acknowledgment is an act in which a document signer personally appears before a notary is identified by the notary and acknow-ledges signing the document.

Fifth - Completing the Notarization

For example, when completing a venue heading for a jurat, a notary shall administer an oath or affirmation to the affiant and shall determine, from satisfactory evidence as described in Section 1185 of the Civil Code, that the affiant is the person executing the document. The affiant shall then sign the document in the presence of the notary (Government Code section 8202).

Upon completion of the notarial certificate, sign by hand, your name exactly as it appears on your notary seal or stamp and affix your notary seal. It is never proper for a Notary to stamp and sign a document that lacks notarial wording, this is improper and meaningless. (Government Code section 8207)

KEEPING DOCUMENTATION OF YOUR NOTORIAL ACTS

Notaries are required to keep a record of all their notarial acts. You are required to maintain a bound notary journal (record book or log), not a loose leaf notebook. Notary journals may be purchased through an office supply store. Journals can be used to jog your memory about a notarization that took place earlier and can be used as evidence if so needed in a court of law. Your journal is your personal property and should not be surrendered to an employer even if you have left their employment. Always safeguard your journal by keeping it in a locked area where you have exclusive access.

You are encouraged to complete your journal before you perform your notarization, so that all the information in your journal is complete before the signer has left your presence.

JURATS AND ACKNOWLEDGEMENTS

A Jurat is the process of taking verification upon oath or affirmation. An example of a jurat would be an affidavit, a deposition, or other sworn document. (Government Code sections 8202 and 8205)

The main purpose of a jurat is to compel document signer's truthfulness.

In a jurat, the notary appeals to the signer's conscience and requires him/her to swear to the truthfulness of the document's content. Then the notary completes the appropriate notarial certificate. Sometimes a jurat (Latin, for *oath) is* executed without reference to a document, as with the oath of office given to a public official.

A jurat is commonly referred to as the "certificate" completed and attached to an affidavit after the notary public has administered an

FAST FACTS:

The main purpose of the notorial act called an acknowledg-ment is to positively identify the signer.

oath or affirmation. (Government Code sections 8202 and 8205)

A jurat guarantees four things about the document signer:

- **IDENTITY**: The signer provided satisfactory evidence of his or her identity to the notary public.

- **SEE**: The signer personally appeared before the notary. *(On the date and in the county indicated)*

- **SWEAR OR AFFIRM**: The notary gave the signer an oath/affirmation. (Oath for a document signer: *"I do solemnly swear that the statements in this document are true, so help me God"*)

  (Affirmation for a document signer: "Do you solemnly affirm, under the penalty of perjury, that the statements made herein are true?")

- **SIGN:** The document was signed in the presence of the notary.

Note: *With recent changes in the laws use of a jurat does require the notary to identify the signer. (See the discussion of "IDENTIFYING Signers" under the section "Acknowledgments" below). (Government Code section 8202).*

If a notary public executes a jurat and the statement sworn or subscribed to is contained in a document purporting to identify the affiant, and includes the birthdate or age of the person and a purported photograph or finger print of the person so swearing or subscribing, the notary public shall require, as a condition to executing the jurat, that the person verify the birthdate or age contained in the statement by showing either:

> (a) A certified copy of the person's birth certificate, or

> (b) An identification card or driver's license issued by the Department of Motor Vehicles.

For the purposes of preparing for submission of forms required by the United States Citizenship and Immigraton Services, and only for such purposes, a notary public may also accept for identification any documents or declarations acceptable to the United States Citizenship and Immigration Services. (Government Code section 8230).

JURAT CERTIFICATE

The certificate shown below contains the basic elements which must be included in every jurat certificate. The jurisdiction is the State where the notarization took place. The **venue** is defined as the location where the notarial act took place. The jurat certificate

FAST FACTS:

Through evidence an acknowledg-ment provides assurance that a signer is not an imposter.

must be attached to all affidavits subscribed and sworn to before a notary public. (Government Code section 8202)

California Drivers License

When executing a jurat, a notary shall administer an oath or affirmation to the affiant and shall determine, from satisfactory evidence as described in Section 1185 of the Civil Code, that the affiant is the person executing the document. The affiant shall sign the document in the presence of the notary. To any affidavit subscribed and sworn to before a notary, there shall be attached a jurat in the following form. (Government Code section 8202(a)(b)).

JURAT CERTIFICATE

> A notary public or other officer completing this certificate verifies only the identity of the individual who signed the document to which this certificate is attached, and not the truthfulness, accuracy, or validity of that document.

State of   (___*California*___)ss

County of   (_____)

Subscribed and sworn to (or affirmed) before me on this

_____ day of _____, 20__, by _____,

proved to me on the basis of satisfactory evidence to be the person(s) who appeared before me.

Witness my hand and official seal.

_____

Notary Public Signature   Seal

ACKNOWLEDGMENTS

(The most common type of notarization)

The *acknowledgment* is an act in which a document signer personally appears before a notary, provides satisfactory evidence of his or her identity. In an effort to help prevent fraud, Tthe constituent must acknowledge previously signing document. The notary certifies that these actions are completed (Civil Code section 1185 and AB 886).

An acknowledgment differs from a jurat as follows: In an oath or affirmation, a person swears to the truthfulness of statements made. In an acknowledgment, a person is **not** swearing to the **truthfulness** of statements. A certificate of acknowledgement is executed under penalty of perjury and any notary public who willfully states as true any material fact that he or she knows to

FAST FACTS:

An expired driver's license that was issued within the past five years is acceptable.

be false shall be subject to a civil penalty not exceeding ten thousand dollars ($10,000). (Civil Code 1189(a)(2).

The main purpose of the notarial act called an acknowledgment is to prove satisfactory evidence of the identity of the signer. Acknowledgments also entitle the instrument to be recorded and provide official evidence of its execution.

An acknowledgment indicates three things about the signer:

The signer **personally appeared** before the notary *(On the date and in the county indicated).*

ID: The signer's **identity was proven** to the notary by satisfactory evidence.

ACKNOWLEDGE: The signer **acknowledged signing** the document *(Document does not have to be signed in the presence of the notary Civil Code section 1189) and California Government Code section 8214.15.*

A notary public or other officer completing this certificate verifies only the identity of the individual who signed the document to which this certificate is attached, and not the truthfulness, accuracy, or validity of that document.

State of   (___ *California* ___)ss

County of   (_____)

On_____before me, (here insert name and title of the officer),   personally appeared_____,   who proved to me on the basis of satisfactory evidence to be the person(s) whose name(s) is/are subscribed to the within instrument and acknowledged to me that he/she/they executed the same in his/her/their authorized capacity(ies), and that by his/her/their signature(s) on the instrument the person(s), or the entity upon behalf of which the person(s) acted, executed the instrument. I certify under PENALTY OF PERJURY under the   laws of the State of California that the foregoing paragraph is true and correct.

WITNESS my hand and official seal.

_____

Notary Public Signature   Seal

FAST FACTS:

All credible witnesses must sign the notary's journal along with the document signer.

The above form must be filled out completely at the time of a notary's signature and seal. Perjury penalties specified under (Civil Code section 1189(a)(1)). Penalties can reach as much as $10,000.

Every person who, having taken an oath that he or she will testify, declare, depose, or certify truly before any competent tribunal, officer, or person, in any of the cases in which the oath may by law of the State of California be administered, willfully and contrary to the oath, states as true any material matter which he or she knows to be false, and every person who testifies, declares, deposes, or certifies under penalty of perjury in any of the cases in which the testimony, declarations, depositions, or certification is permitted by law of the State of California under penalty of perjury and willfully states as true any material matter which he or she knows to be false, is guilty of perjury. This subdivision is applicable whether the statement, or the testimony, declaration, deposition, or certification is made or subscribed within or without the State of California.

Perjury is punishable by imprisonment pursuant to subdivision (h) of Section 1170 for two, three or four years. (Penal Code sections 118 and 126)

In an effort to facilitate interstate commerce, California now allows its notaries to complete acknowledgment certificates from other states for documents that will be recorded in another state or jurisdiction of the United States as long as the notary does not make a determination of the representative capacity in which a person signs the document. Acknowledgments on documents that will be recorded in another country must be in the form prescribed in Civil Code section 1189. (Civil Code section 1189(c)) [As an example the text would read: "... personally appeared Jane Doe, **who acknowledged to me** that she was the President of ACME Widget Company... "If the wording differs, and the document will be recorded in California or outside of the United States, a loose certificate of acknowledgment with the statutory wording must be used. (Civil Code section 1189(a))

Notaries should always keep in mind that you can never notarize an incomplete document. If you know from experience that a document is incomplete or if it appears to be incomplete do not notarize the document.

IDENTIFYING "Signers" (Civil Code section 1185, and Government Code section 8202)

Notaries can be investigated for unethical and criminal behavior.

FAST FACTS:

A credible witness may be used if a document signer is unable to obtain proper ID within the time frame of the transaction.

In these cases notaries that aid and abet fraud by loaning their journal to a non-notary, by notarizing documents without all of the parties present or by failing to properly secure their journal and stamp can now more easily be investigated and prosecuted.

If identity was established by satisfactory evidence pursuant to Section 1185 of the Civil Code, the journal shall contain the signature of the credible witness swearing or affirming to the identity of the individual or the type of identifying document, the governmental agency issuing the document, the serial or identifying number of the document, and the date of issue or expiration of the document. (Government Code section 8206(D)).

If the identity of the person making the acknowledgment or taking the oath or affirmation was established by the oaths or affirmations of two credible witnesses whose identities are proven to the notary public by presentation of any document satisfying the requirements of Section 1185 of the Civil Code, the notary public shall record in the journal the type of documents identifying the witnesses, the identifying numbers on the documents identifying the witnesses, and the dates of issuance or expiration of the documents identifying the witnesses. (Government Code section 8206(E)).

Through evidence an acknowledgment provides assurance that a signer is not an impostor trying to profit from a phony document. The notary identifies a constituent who "acknowledges" having signed the document.

In taking acknowledgments, the constituent must:

Prove on the basis of satisfactory evidence

"Satisfactory evidence" means the absence of any information, evidence, or other circumstances which would lead a reasonable person to believe that the person making the acknowledgment is not the individual he or she claims to be and any of the following:

(1) The oath or affirmation of a **credible** witness personally known to the officer….(2) The oath or affirmation under penalty of perjury of two credible witnesses, whose identities are proven to the notary by the presentation of satisfactory evidence,…..(3) Reasonable reliance on the presentation of any one of the following……(please see list of acceptable IDs below)The notary does not verify the **capacity** in **which** a person signs—such as corporate officer, trustee, partner to a partnership etc. The notary only identifies the acknowledging **signer.**

IDENTIFICATION DOCUMENTS (ID CARDS)

FAST FACTS:

A physical description is not required for a passport.

A notary may identify a document signer through any one of the identification documents listed below. The document must:

- Be current, or if expired, issued within the past five years.

- Bear a serial number or other identifying number.

ACCEPTABLE ID's

- **California driver's license or non-driver ID** issued by the California Dept. of Motor Vehicles.

- **U.S. passport** *(Physical description not required)*.

- **A passport must be stamped by the U.S. Immigration and Naturalization Service or the U.S. Citizenship and Immigration Services (recent name change) (Civil Code section 1185(b)(4)).**

- **Driver's license or non-driver ID issued by another U.S. State.**

- **Drivers' license issued in Mexico or Canada.**

- **U.S. military ID. The ID must have a photo, description, signature and official ID number.**

- **Inmates can also use their inmate ID approved by the California Department of Corrections and Rehabilitation (CDRC) if performing a notarized signature in prison.**

- **An employee identification card issued by an agency or office of the State of California, or by an agency or office of a city, county, or city and county in this state. (Civil Code section 1185(f))**

Again, remember that the above documents must be current or have been issued within the last five years, contain a description of the person presenting it and a photograph, signature, ID number, issuing agency.

You must see one of these identification cards.
"Combining"
cards to obtain the proper information is not acceptable.

ID CARDS WITH LIMITED ACCEPTABILITY

Inmate ID issued by the California Department of Corrections (only *used to identify prisoners in custody).*

Resident Alien ID, or "green card," issued by the U.S. Immigration and Naturalization Service (USCIS), **but only for**

FAST FACTS:

A Social Security Card is not an acceptable form of identification for notarizations

notarizing Jurats of *USCIS* **forms (Government Code section 8230). Summary: "Green Cards" are not good ID.**

Unacceptable ID cards for identifying Signers: Social Security cards, birth certificates, credit cards and driver's licenses without photographs.

California law requires only one identification card to determine identity. However, it may be prudent to ask for more than one card if the Notary has any doubt as to the validity of the card.

CREDIBLE WITNESS

If identification cannot be established from satisfactory identification, you may rely on the oath or affirmation of one credible witness to identify an unknown constituent. (Civil Codes sections 1185(b)(1)(A)(i through v)).

A credible witness *(one or* two)**, must swear or affirm the following:**

- The person making the acknowledgment is the person named in the document.

- The witness personally knows the person making the acknowledgment.

- That it is the reasonable belief of the witness that it is **very difficult** or **impossible** for the person making the acknowledgment to obtain satisfactory identification within the time frame of the transaction.

- The person making the acknowledgment does not possess any of the acceptable identification documents.

- The witness does not have a **financial or beneficial** interest in the transaction and is **not named in the document.**

OATH OR AFFIRMATION GIVEN TO TWO CREDIBLE WITNESSES

Do you solemnly swear *that the (person making the acknowledgment)* is the person named in the document; that *(person making the acknowledgment)* is personally known to you; that it is your reasonable belief that the circumstances of *(person making acknowledgment)* are such that it would be very **difficult** or **impossible** for him or her to obtain a satisfactory form of identification within the time frame of this transaction; that *(person making the acknowledgment)* does not possess any of the acceptable identification documents; and that you do not have a financial or beneficial interest nor are you named in the

FAST FACTS:

There is no California law prohibiting a notary from notarizing immigration documents.

document being acknowledged, so help you God? OR

Do you solemnly affirm, under the penalties of perjury, that the (person making the acknowledgement) is the person named in the document; that (person making the acknowledgement) is personally know to you; that it is your reasonable belief that the circumstances of (person making acknowledgement) are such that it would be very difficult or impossible for him or her to obtain a satisfactory form of identification within the time frame of this transaction; that (person making the acknowledgement) does not possess any of the acceptable identification documents; and that you do not have a financial or beneficial interest nor are you named in the document being acknowledged, upon your honor?

An individual's signature or subscription includes a mark. When a person cannot write his name, he may sign with an "X" or another mark that is witnessed by 2 witnesses who must subscribe their own names as witnesses on the document (Civil Code 14).

PROOF BY SUBSCRIBING WITNESS

A SPECIAL TYPE OF ACKNOWLEDGMENT

When the signer of an instrument is unable to appear before a notary to acknowledge its execution, a subscribing witness may make proof of execution (Code of Civil Procedure section 1195).

HOWEVER, SECURITY AGREEMENTS, AND GRANT DEEDS (OTHER THAN TRUSTEE'S DEEDS OR DEEDS OF RECONVEYANCE), QUITCLAIM DEEDS, MORTGAGES, DEEDS OF TRUST, AND POWERS OF ATTORNEY CANNOT BE RECORDED IF PROVED BY SUBSCRIBING WITNESS (Civil Code section 1195(b)) (Government Code section 27287).

REQUIREMENTS FOR A SUBSCRIBING WITNESS

A subscribing witness is one who sees a writing executed or hears it acknowledged, and at the request of the party thereupon signs his name as a witness. He or she must also be able to state that the principal requested that the subscribing witness sign the document as a witness; that the subscribing witness signed the document as a witness, and both the subscribing witness and credible witness must sign the notary's journal. (California Code of Civil Procedure section 1935; Government Code section 8206; and Civil Code section 1195). Additionally, the subscribing witness must be identified by the oath of a credible witness (who must be personally known to the notary

FAST FACTS:

The Notary Public Institute recommends that you provide your constituent with a receipt if one is requested.

and the subscribing witness) and provides the officer with any document satisfying the requirements of Section 1185. (Civil Code section 1195).

If a person called the principal, has signed a document, but does not personally appear before a notary public, another person can appear on the principal's behalf to prove the principal signed (or "executed") the document. That person is called a subscribing witness. (Code of Civil Procedure section 1935)

A proof of execution by a subscribing witness cannot be used in conjunction with any quitclaim deed, grant deed (other than a trustee's deed or deed of reconveyance), mortgage, deed of trust, or security agreement. A subscribing witness appearing before a notary public on behalf of another person (principal) cannot be used on powers of attorney or any other documents requiring a notary public to obtain a thumbprint in the notary public journal from the party signing the document (Government Code section 27287 and Civil Code section 1195(b)) (1) and (2)

The requirements for proof of execution by a subscribing witness are as follows:

- The subscribing witness must prove (say under oath) that the person who signed the document as a party, the principal, is the person described in the document, and the subscribing witness personally knows the principal (Civil Code section 1197); and

- The subscribing witness must say, under oath, that the subscribing witness was requested by the principal to sign the document as a witness and that the subscribing witness did so (code of Civil Procedure 1935 and Civil Code section 1197; and Code of Civil Procedure section 1935)

- The notary public must establish the identity of the subscribing witness by the oath of a credible witness whom the notary personally knows and who personally knows the subscribing witness. The credible witness must also present to the notary public any identification document satisfying the requirements for satisfactory evidence as described in Civil Code section 1185(b)(3) or (4). (Civil Code section 1196); and

- The subscribing witness must sign the notary public's official journal. The credible witness must sign the notary public's official journal or the notary public must record

FAST FACTS:

When one credible witness is used he/she must be personally known by the notary public. and he or she must possess valid ID.(Civil Code section 1185)

in the notary public's official journal the type of identification document presented, the governmental agency issuing the document, the serial number of the document, and the date of expiration of the document (Government Code section 8206(a)(2)(C) and (D)).

Note: The identity of the subscribing witness must be established by the oath of a credible witness who personally knows the subscribing witness and who is personally known by the notary public. In addition, the credible witness must present an identification document satisfying the requirements of Civil Code section 1185(b)(3)or (4).

SUBSCRIBING WITNESS EXAMPLE

Because proof of execution by a subscribing witness is not commonly used, the following scenario is provided as an example of how proof by a subscribing witness may be used.:

The principal, Paul, needs to have his signature on a document notarized but cannot appear before a notary public because Paul is in the hospital . So Paul asks a long time friend, Sue, to visit the hospital and act as a subscribing witness. When Sue comes to the hospital, Sue must watch Paul sign the document. If Paul has signed the document prior to Sue's arrival Paul must say to Sue that he signed the document. Then Paul should ask Sue to sign the document as a subscribing witness and Sue must do so.

Next, Sue must take the document to a notary public. Sue must bring a credible witness with her to the notary public. Sue chooses Carl a long time friend, as a credible witness because Carl has worked with Nancy the notary public for several years. Therefore, Carl can act as Sue's credible witness.

Sue and Carl appear together before Nancy. Nancy determines she personally knows Carl and also examines Carl's California Driver's License to establish Carl's identity. Then Nancy puts Carl under oath. Under oath, Carl swears that he personally knows Sue, that Sue is the person who signed the document as a subscribing witness, and Carl does not have a financial or beneficial interest in the document signed by Paul and subscribed by Sue. Then Nancy puts Sue under oath. Under Oath Sue swears that she personally knows Paul, that Paul is the person described in the document, that Sue watched Paul sign the document or

FAST FACTS:

The credible witnesses must sign the notary public's official journal and the notary public must record in the notary public's official journal the type of identification document presented.

heard Paul acknowledge Paul signed the document, that Paul requested Sue sign the document as subscribing witness and that Sue did so.

Sue signs Nancy's notary journal as a subscribing witness. Carl must sign Nancy's notary journal as a credible witness, or Nancy must record in Nancy's notary journal the type of identification Carl presented, the governmental issuing agency issuing the document, the serial number of the document, and the date of issue or expiration date of the document.

Nancy completes Nancy's notary public journal entry. Nancy then completes a Proof of Execution Certificate and attaches the Proof of Execution Certificate to the document. Sue takes the notarized document back to Paul.

OATH FOR A SUBSCRIBING WITNESS

Do you solemnly swear that you saw (name principal) sign his/her name to this document (or that principal acknowledged to you that he/she executed the document for the purposes therein stated) and that (name of principal) requested that you subscribe your name to the instrument as a witness, so help you God?

Do you solemnly affirm, under penalty of perjury, that you saw (name of principal) sign his/her name to this document (or that the principal acknowledged to you that he/she executed the document for the purposes therein stated) and that (name of principal) requested that you subscribe your name to the instrument as a witness, upon your honor?Subscribing Witness Certificate:

State of _____*California*_____ss

County of _____

On ____ (date), before me, the undersigned, a notary public for the state, personally appeared ____ (name of subscribing witness), proved to me to be the person whose name is subscribed to the within instrument, as a witness thereto, on the oath of ____ (name of credible witness), a credible witness who is known to me and provided a satisfactory identifying document. ____ (name of subscribing witness), being by me duly sworn, said that he/she was present and saw/heard ____ (name[s] of principal[s]), the same person (s) described in and whose

FAST FACTS:

No notary shall receive a fee for performing any official notorial duties on behalf of a veteran regarding service, discharge, separation, pension, insurance, compensation or any other service in connection with the above (Government code section 8211(f)).

name(s) is/are subscribed to the within or attached instrument in his/her/their authorized capacity(ies) as (a) party(ies) thereto, execute or acknowledge executing the same, and that said affiant subscribed his/her name to the within or attached instrument as a witness at the request of _____ (name[s] of principal[s]).

WITNESS my hand and official seal.

_____

Notary Public Signature   Seal

(The "all-purpose " Acknowledgment Certificate should not be used for accepting proof of execution by subscribing witnesses. County recorders will reject "all-purpose " certificates that are used improperly. Always use the correct certificate for the act that you are performing.)

FAST FACTS:

A credible witness must present an identification document satisfying the requirements of Civil Code section 1185(b)(3)or (4).

Chapter 3

TEST YOUR KNOWLEDGE

1) The main purpose of a jurat is to compel the document signer's truthfulness.

     a) True

     b) False

2) A jurat can easily be spotted because of the wording "subscribed and sworn to" on the face of the document.

     a) True

     b) False

3) The main purpose of an acknowledgment is to positively identify the signer.

     a) True

     b) False

4) Notaries can accept expired identification documents as long as they were issued within the past five years.

     a) True

     b) False

5) Combining identification cards to obtain the proper information is an acceptable practice.

     a) True

     b) False

6) An acknowledgment does not guarantee that the signer signed in the presence of a notary.

     a) True

     b) False

7) A jurat guarantees that a constituent signed in the presence of a notary.

     a) True

     b) False

8) In an acknowledgment and a jurat the notary certifies that the signer was positively identified.

     a) True

     b) False

9) It is okay to notarize documents for a member of your family.

     a) True

     b) False

10) There are no exceptions to the rule that a California notary must use his or her seal for all official acts.

     a) True

     b) False

Chapter 4

The Notary Journal and Tools of the Trade

California law says a notary public is required to keep a sequential journal of all acts performed as a notary public (Government Code section *8206*). *A notary is only permitted one journal in use at any one time. (Government Code section 8206(a)(1)).* The journal shall be kept in a locked and secured area, under the direct and exclusive control of the notary. Failure to secure the journal shall be cause for the Secretary of State to take administrative action against the commission held by the notary public.(Government Code section 8206(a)(1) and 8214.1).

In addition to being a legal requirement, there are *at least four additional reasons* why keeping a journal is a good practice:

1. The journal can serve as an excellent form of legal protection for the notary.

2. If a notary certificate is lost or damaged, a notary can refer to the journal entry to verify the prior existence of the certificate.

3. If a notary is called upon to testify in a legal proceeding, the journal provides the ideal reminder of the facts and circumstances surrounding the notarization in question.

4. If notarization is denied or refused the entry can so indicate.The entry into the journal indicates a record of denial.

In an effort to help safeguard the integrity of your journal you should be aware that any person who solicits, coerces, or in any manner influences a notary public to perform an improper notarial act shall be guilty of a misdemeanor. Prosecution for this offense shall be commenced within 4 years of the offense or the discovery or within 4 years after the completion of the offense (Government Code section 8225).

The journal is the exclusive property of the notary and cannot be surrendered to another person, except to the county clerk or to a peace officer, even if this individual paid for the journal. (Government Code sections 8206 and 8209)

"THE JOURNAL BECOMES YOUR BEST FRIEND"

The record shall include: (Government Code section 8206)

- *Date, time* and *type* of each official act. (e.g., acknowledgement, jurat)

- *Character* of every instrument acknowledged or proved before the notary. (e.g., deed of trust, powers of attorney)

FAST FACTS:

The journal can serve as an excellent form of legal protection for the notary.

- The *signature* of each person whose signature is being notarized.

- Identity must be established by satisfactory evidence pursuant to (Civil Code section 1185), then the journal shall contain the signature of the credible witness swearing or affirming to the identity of the individual or the type of identifying document, the governmental agency issuing the document, the serial or identifying number of the document, and the date of issue or expiration of the document.

- If the identity of the person making the acknowledgment was established by the oaths or affirmations of two credible witnesses whose identities are proven upon the presentation of satisfactory evidence, the type of identifying documents, the identifying numbers of the documents and the dates of Issuance or expiration of the documents presented by the witnesses to establish their identity.

- Record the *fee* charged for the notarial service.

- Same special circumstances: If the document to be notarized is a **deed, quitclaim deed,** or **deed of trust** affecting real property, *the notary public shall require the party signing the document to place his or her right thumbprint in the journal.* A thumbprint is also required in the journal for a power of attorney document (Government Code section 8206(G)). The law also requires a party signing any document affecting real property to place his or her thumbprint in the notary public's journal. This does not apply to a trustee's deed resulting from a decree of foreclosure or a non-judicial foreclosure pursuant to Civil Code section 2924, or to a deed of re-conveyance. If the right thumbprint is not available, then the notary shall have the party use his or her left thumb or any available finger and shall so indicate in the journal. If the party signing the document is physically unable to provide a thumb or fingerprint, the notary shall so indicate in the journal and shall also provide an explanation of that physical condition. This paragraph shall not apply to a trustee's deed resulting from a decree of foreclosure or a non-judicial foreclosure pursuant to (Civil Code section 2924) , nor to a deed of reconveyance.

- A notary public who fails to obtain a thumbprint, as required by Section 8206, from a party signing a document shall be subject to a civil penalty not exceeding two thousand five

FAST FACTS:

If the party signing the documents is physically unable to provide a thumb or fingerprint, the notary shall indicate so in the journal and provide an explanation of that physical condition.

hundred dollars ($2,500). An action to impose a civil penalty under this subdivision may be brought by the Secretary of State in an administrative proceeding or any public prosecutor in superior court, and shall be enforced as a civil judgment. A public prosecutor shall inform the secretary of any civil penalty imposed under this section (Government Code section 8214.23).

• If a sequential journal of official acts performed by a notary public is stolen, lost, misplaced, destroyed, damaged, or otherwise rendered unusable as a record of notarial acts and information, the notary public shall immediately notify the Secretary of State by certified or registered mail. The notification shall include the period of the journal entries, the notary public commission number, the expiration date of the commission and when applicable, a photocopy of any police report that specifies the theft of the sequential journal of official acts. (Government Code section 8206(b)).

• Upon written request of any member of the public, (request to include the name of the parties, the type of document and the month and year in which notarized), the notary shall supply a photostatic copy of the line item representing the requested transaction within 15 business days after receipt of request at a cost of not more than 30 cents per page or you must acknowledge that the information doesn't exist. (Government Code sections 8206(c) and 8206.5)

A notary public who is an employee shall permit inspection and copying of journal transactions by a duly designated auditor or agent of the notary public's employer, provided that the inspection and copying is done in the presence of the notary public and the transactions are directly associated with the business purposes of the employer. (Government Code section 8206(d)).

THE NOTORIAL JOURNAL

All notaries public must keep and maintain a notarial journal. Any notary public that willfully fails to perform his or her duty relating to the official journal control under section 8206 [relating to the official journal], is guilty of a misdemeanor (Government Code section 8228.1).

The Notary Public Institute recommends that the information contained in the front of the notarial journal be kept current. This includes the notary public's name, notarial commission number, expiration date, address, etc. Effective January 1, 2006, the Notary Public Institute recommends made it a misdemeanor for a notary public to willfully fail to properly maintain his or her notorial journal.

FAST FACTS:

The journal reminds a notary to ask for necessary information and provides a reason to get that information if the client is reluctant.

As a notarial commission is renewed or a notary public moves from one employer to another, the Notary Public Institute recommends that this information be updated. A notary public must keep only one active sequential journal containing all acts performed as a notary public at a time (Government Code section 8206). Any notary public that willfully fails to perform any duty required of a notary including failing to properly maintain his or her journal, (2) willfully fails to notify the Secretary of State if his or her journal is lost or stolen, rendered unusable or surrendered to a peace officer, (3) willfully fails to permit a lawful inspection or copying of his or her notarial journal, (4) willfully fails to keep his or her seal under the direct and exclusive control, or (5) willfully fails to keep his or her notarial seal to any person not authorized to possess it is guilty of a misdemeanor. (Government Code section 8228.1)

IMPORTANCE OF THE JOURNAL

The notarial journal is a vital component of exercising reasonable care. It is prudent to diligently keep a record of your notarial transactions. If anyone wishes to make inquiries about a notarization, few people can trust their memory to perfectly recall the incident, and fewer still would accept something that wasn't written down.

The journal reminds a notary to ask for necessary information and provides a reason to get that information if the client is reluctant. It serves as evidence that your side of the story is true. Most of the time it can prevent a notary from being named in a suit. The Secretary of State relies on journal entries when a complaint has been lodged against a notary.

If it is necessary to alter a notarial certificate, the journal can help to verify the point in question. Of course, it is also the place of record that the correction was made.

In the final analysis, of course, you need to keep a journal properly because it is the law. Statutes require a notarial journal, and state law specifies what must be kept in the journal.

Complete the journal BEFORE the certificate-"Get what you need before they get what they want."

Remember the steps:

    • Screen the Signer.

    • Jot it in the Journal.

    • Complete the Certificate..

RECORD EVERYTHING

FAST FACTS:

California law specifically requires that a notary use a seal "with the exception of subdivision maps."

PUBLIC RECORD

Because the notary public is an officer of the state and is responsible to the public, the notarial journal falls under the public record disclosure laws. Notary law has established that notaries must provide photocopies of line items within the journal if the notary receives a written request to do so (Government Code section 8206(c)).

Notaries are forbidden to disclose their entire journal contents, unless requested by the Secretary of State, It shall further be the duty of a notary public, upon written request:

(1) Upon written notice, the notary public must furnish the Secretary of State certified copies of the notary public's journal by the time specified in the notice. (Government Code section 8205(b)(1))

(2) To respond within 30 days of receiving written requests sent by certified mail from the Secretary of State's office for information relating to official acts performed by the notary. (Government Code section 8205(b)(1)(2)).

The notary public shall not surrender the journal to any other person, except the county clerk, pursuant to Section 8209, or immediately, or if the journal is not present then as soon as possible, upon request to a peace officer investigating a criminal offense who has reasonable suspicion to believe the journal contains evidence of a criminal offense, as defined in Sections 830.1, 830.2, and 830.3 of the Penal Code, acting in his or her official capacity and within his or her authority. If the peace officer seizes the notary journal, he or she must have probable cause as required by the laws of this state and the United States. A peace officer or law enforcement agency that seizes a notary journal shall notify the Secretary of State by facsimile within 24 hours, or as soon as possible thereafter, of the name of the notary public whose journal has been seized. The notary public shall obtain a receipt for the journal, and shall notify the Secretary of State by certified mail within 10 days that the journal was relinquished to a peace officer. (Government Code section 8206(d))

The notary public shall provide the journal for examination and copying in the presence of the notary public upon receipt of a subpoena duces tecum or a court order, and shall certify those copies if requested. (Government Code section 8206(e)).

A notary public who willfully fails to provide access to the sequential journal of notarial acts when requested by a peace officer shall be subject to a civil penalty not exceeding two thousand five hundred dollars ($2,500). An action to impose a civil

FAST FACTS:

California subdivision map certificates may be notarized without the official seal.

penalty under this subdivision may be brought by the Secretary of State in an administrative proceeding or any public prosecutor in superior court, and shall be enforced as a civil judgment. A public prosecutor shall inform the secretary of any civil penalty imposed under this section (Government Code section 8214.21).

DISPOSITION OF RECORDS

The notary public must retain the journal until his or her commission is no longer active and then it should be surrendered to the County Clerk. Since it is the only record of the notarization and because the statute of limitations is uncertain, the Secretary of State encourages permanent storage. (Government Code section 8228.1). Whether or not a notary kept the journal for a limited time, the Secretary of State must have a record of the place the journal is currently being stored (Government Code section 8206).

The journal of notarial acts of a notary public is the exclusive property of that notary public, and shall not be surrendered to an employer upon termination of employment.

(a) If any notary public resigns, is disqualified, removed from office, or allows his or her appointment to expire without obtaining reappointment within 30 days, all notarial records and papers shall be delivered within 30 days to the clerk of the county in which the notary public's current official oath of office is on file. If the notary public willfully fails or refuses to deliver all notarial records and papers to the county clerk within 30 days, the person is guilty of a misdemeanor and shall be personally liable for damages to any person injured by that action or inaction. (Government Code section 8206(d))

(b) In the case of the death of a notary public, the personal representative of the deceased shall promptly notify the Secretary of State of the death of the notary public and shall deliver all notarial records and papers of the deceased to the clerk of the county in which the notary public's official oath of office is on file.

(c) After 10 years from the date of deposit with the county clerk, if no request for, or reference to such records has been made, they may be destroyed upon order of court. (Government Code section 8209)

If a notary public willfully fails or refuses to deliver all notarial records and papers to the county clerk within 30 days [of resignation, removal from office, or commission expiration], the person is guilty of a misdemeanor and shall be personally liable for

FAST FACTS:

The Secretary of State will issue a "Certificate of Authorization" so that you can purchase a notary stamp.

damages to any person injured by that action or inaction (Government Code section 8209(a)).

THE OFFICIAL NOTARY SEAL

Is a notarial seal necessary?

California law specifically requires that a notary use a seal (Government Code section 8207). Because of the legal requirement that the seal be photographically reproducible, the rubber stamp seal has become almost universal. Many documents, which are acknowledged, may later be recorded. The recorder may not accept a document if the notary seal is illegible or in red ink – the notary public must use black or blue ink.

The seal should not be placed over signatures or any printed matter on the document. An illegible or improperly placed seal may result in rejection of the document for recordation and result in inconveniences and extra expenses for all those involved. (Government Code sections 8202 and 8207 and Civil Code sections 1189 and 1195)

If the document to be notarized does not contain the proper wording or does not allow for enough space to complete the notarization, a certificate can be attached to the document to complete the notarization.

Additionally, any person that knowingly destroys, defaces, or conceals any records or papers belonging to the office of a notary public shall be guilty of a misdemeanor and shall be liable in a civil action for damages to any person injured as a result of such destruction, defacing or concealment (Government Code section 8221).

The legal requirements for a rubber stamp seal stipulate that the seal must (Government Code section 8207):

1. Be photographically reproducible when it is affixed to a document *(an embossment seal would have to be smudged or darkened to be picked up by a copier).*

2. Conform to the following dimensions: *Circular:* Not over two inches in diameter. *Rectangular:* Not more than one inch in width by two and one-half inches in length

3. Contain the *State Seal* and the words "Notary Public."

4. Contain the *name* of the notary public.

5. Contain the *name of the county* where the oath of office and notary bond is on file.

6. It must contain the *expiration date* of the notary public

FAST FACTS:

Your notarial seal must be locked up when not in use and must be under your direct and exclusive control.

commission.

7. Contain the *sequential identification number* assigned to the notary and the identification number assigned to the manufacturer or vendor.

8. Have a serrated or milled-edged border.

An example of a rectangular stamp with the required elements appears below:

CHRIS MORGAN
Comm. #0000000
NOTARY PUBLIC – CALIFORNIA
Santa Cruz County
My Comm. Expires April 15, 2021

EXCEPTION: In California, the law allows one condition under which a notary does not have to use a seal. Since subdivision maps are usually drawn on a material that will not accept standard stamp pad ink and other acceptable inks are not as readily available, acknowledgments for California **subdivision maps** may be notarized without the official seal (Government Code section 66436(c)). The notary's name the county of the notary's principal place of business and the commission expiration date must be typed or printed below or immediately adjacent to the notary's signature on the acknowledgment.

Where may a notary obtain a seal?

Seals *(and stamps)* may be purchased from authorized stationers and tool and die makers. Please obtain a list of approved vendors from the Secretary of State. (Government Code section 8207.3). the Secretary of State will issue you a "certificate of authorization" so that you can purchase a notary stamp. A certificate of authorization to manufacture a notary public seal will be included with the commission packet once the Secretary of State has commissioned the notary public. (Government Code section 8207.2-(d)). The State of California does not offer notarial seals for sale.

The seal may either be circular, not more than two inches in diameter, or rectangular, not more than one inch in height and two and one-half inches in length. The seal must imprint or emboss a photographically reproducible impression.

If your seal is lost, misplaced, destroyed, broken or damaged, you must immediately mail or deliver written notice to the Secretary of State. To replace your seal, you must request a new certificate of authorization, and one will be sent to you.

FAST FACTS:

The seal must be destroyed if no longer valid i.e. terminated, resignation, or revocation of the notary's commission (California Government Code section 8207).

Failure to report can result in a $1,500.00 fines (Government Code section 8207.3(e)). When your commission is no longer valid, destroy your seal.

As of January 1, 2006, the law made it a misdemeanor for a notary public to willfully fail to keep his or her seal under direct and exclusive control (Government Code section 8228.1)

A notary public shall not use the official seal or the title "notary public" for any purpose other than the rendering of notarial service

The law requires that your seal be locked up when not in use and kept in a secure area under the direct and exclusive control of the notary public (Government Code section 8207 and 8214.1).

The notary public's seal cannot be surrendered to another person, except to a court by order of that court, even if this individual paid for the seal (Government Code section 8207). The notary's official seal can only be used for rendering notarial services.

The seal must be destroyed if no longer valid i.e. terminated, resignation, or revocation (Government Code section 8207).

FAST FACTS:

The law requires that your seal be locked up when not in use and kept in a secure area under the direct and exclusive control of the notary public (Government Code section 8207 and 8214.1).

Chapter 4

TEST YOUR KNOWLEDGE

1)   Maintaining multiple journals is acceptable as long as they are all kept under lock and key when not in use.
    a) True
    b) False

2)   Notaries must retain their journals in locked and secure areas under the direct and exclusive control of the notary.
    a) True
    b) False

3)   California law requires that notary seals must be photographically reproducible when affixed to a document.
    a) True
    b) False

4)   The notary stamp must include the notary's social security number.
    a) True
    b) False

5)   If your seal is lost, misplaced, destroyed, broken or damaged, you must notify the secretary of state immediately.
    a) True
    b) False

6)   Never use white-out to make corrections to certificates or entries in your journal.
    a) True
    b) False

7)   If there is no room for a notary seal on the document it may be affixed on a completed certificate.
    a) True
    b) False

8)   A notary seal that is not legible may be corrected by re-affixing the seal in an area adjacent to the illegible seal.
    a) True
    b) False

9)   Failure to provide access to your sequential journal of notarial acts when requested by a peace officer shall be subject to a civil penalty not exceeding $2,500.
    a) True
    b) False

10)   Failure to obtain a thumbprint, as required by section 8206, from a party signing a document shall be subject to a civil penalty not exceeding $2,500.
    a) True
    b) False

Chapter 5

Notary Shield – Protecting Yourself

It is not possible to be protected from a lawsuit, but you can reduce its effects. There are two ways to deal with lawsuits against notaries: reduce what it costs if you lose or win the suit altogether.

FILING OF THE NOTARY PUBLIC BOND AND OATH OF OFFICE

Once the commission has been issued, a person has 30 calendar days from the beginning of the term prescribed in the commission to take, subscribe, and file an oath of office and file a $15,000 surety bond with the county clerk's office. The commission does not take effect until the oath and bond are filed with the county clerk's office. The filing must take place in the county where the notary public maintains a principal place of business as shown in the application on file with the Secretary of State.

If the oath and bond are not filed within the 30-calendar-day time period, the commission will not be valid, and the person commissioned may not act as a notary public until a new appointment is obtained and the person has properly qualified within the 30-calendar-day time limit. Government Code section 8213(a) permits the filing of completed oaths and bonds by the applicable county clerk by certified mail. Exceptions are not made to the 30-day filing requirement due to mail service delays, county clerk mail processing delays, or for any other reason. If mailing an oath and bond to the county clerk, sufficient time must be allowed by the newly appointed notary public to ensure timely filing. (Government Code sections 8212 and 8213)

BONDING VS INSURANCE

California law requires all notaries to have and post a bond in the amount of $15,000. Remember that errors and omissions insurance protects the notary from the public, and a bond protects the public from the notary.

ERRORS AND OMISSIONS INSURANCE

Errors and omissions insurance covers a notary if he or she is sued over the performance of a notarization. If a notary is sued, the insurance company will handle the litigation, bringing in expertise that the average person is hard-pressed to match. The company will negotiate a settlement if it finds a compelling reason to do so. Of course, it will pay the amount against the defendant up to the limit of the policy. However, there are two

FAST FACTS:

California law requires all notaries public to have and post a bond in the amount of $15,000.

overriding factors that reduce the usefulness of this insurance.

First is the payoff ceiling. By its very nature, insurance will only pay assessed damages up to a certain amount. Most standard policies don't go over $100,000. Yet the liability has no limit. Notaries can be and have been sued for millions of dollars. Obviously, a notary cannot rely on insurance as an adequate safety net.

The second limitation is that errors and omission insurance covers only what the insurance company determines is accidental, or negligent misconduct. If a court determines that the misconduct was intentional, even if not done with criminal intent, the notary may not be covered at all.

Notaries public and their sureties on the notary public's official bond are liable in a civil action to the persons injured for all damages sustained from the notary public's misconduct or neglect. If damages exceed the amount of the notary's official bond the notary public is liable for the remaining balance of the liability (Government Code section 8214).

IMMIGRATION /FOREIGN LANGUAGE

There is no California law prohibiting a notary from notarizing immigration documents. As a non-attorney notary public you cannot assist a client in entering data on immigration forms unless the notary is also a qualified and bonded immigration consultant. However, any notary public may perform notarizations on immigration documents (Government Code sections 8205 and 8223).

TRANSLATIONS

Every notary public who is not an attorney who advertises the services of a notary public in a language other than English by signs or other means of written communication, with the exception of a single desk plaque, shall post with that advertisement a notice in English and in the other language which sets forth the following:

(1) This statement: I am not an attorney and, therefore, cannot give legal advice about immigration or any other legal matters.

(2) The fees are set by statute which a notary public may charge.

(b) The notice required by subdivision (a) shall be printed and posted as prescribed by the Secretary of State.

FAST FACTS:

Subscribing witness vouches for the genuineness of the signature of a signer who does not appear before the notary.

(c) Literal translation of the phrase "notary public" into Spanish, hereby defined as "notario publico" or "notario," is prohibited.

(d) The Secretary of State shall suspend for a period of not less than one year or revoke the commission of any notary public who fails to comply with subdivision (a) or (c). However, on the second offense the commission of such notary public shall be revoked permanently.(Government Code section 8219.5).

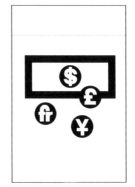

FEES FOR NOTARIAL SERVICES

A notary may charge a fee for notarial service up to and including the following maximum fees as set by law. <u>In no case may a notary charge more than the maximum fee.</u>

In addition to the above fee schedule no fee may be charged to a United States military veteran for notarization of an application or claim for a pension, allotment, allowance, compensation, insurance or any other veteran's benefit (Government Code sections 8203.6, 8211 & 6107. Keep in mind that as a notary public you are not required to charge a fee for your services. You may choose to charge less than the maximum allowable fee but you can not more than the maximum fee as established by law (Government Code section 6100). Non-attorney notaries public that serve as immigration consultants may not charge more than $15.00 for entering data provided by the client on immigration forms (Government Code section 8223).

Section 1 Maximum Fees Allowed

The maximum fees that a notary public may charge are:

ACKNOWLEDGMENTS - $15

For taking an acknowledgment or **proof** of a **deed,** or other instrument, to include the seal and the writing of the certificate, the sum of $15 dollars for each signature taken. (Government Code section 8211). For example, for notarizing a single document with signatures of three persons appearing before the notary a maximum fee of $30 could be charged (Government Code section 8211(a)).

JURATS - $15

For administering an oath or affirmation to one person and executing the jurat, including the seal, the sum is $10 dollars (Government Code section 8211(b)).

FAST FACTS:

In no case may a notary charge more than the maximum fee.

DEPOSITIONS - $30

For all services rendered in connection with the taking of any deposition, the sum of $30, and in addition thereto, the sum of $7 for administering the oath to the witness and the sum of $7 for the certificate to such deposition. (Government Code section 8211(c)).

CERTIFIED COPIES

1) A notary can only certify copies of powers of attorney under California Probate Code section 4307 and his or her notary public journal when requested by the Secretary of State, or upon receipt of a subpoena duces tecum or a court order.

2) A notary for providing a certified copy of a power of attorney may charge a maximum of $15.00 per copy. (Government Code section 8211(e)).

JOURNAL ENTRIES (NON CERTIFIED) COPIES

Upon written request of any member of the public, which request shall include the name of the parties, the type of document, and the month and year in which notarized, the notary shall supply a photostatic copy of the line item representing the requested transaction at a cost of not more than thirty cents ($0.30) per page (Government Code section 8206(a). The notary has 15 business days from receipt of written request to provide the requested photocopy or an explanation for the delay.

Section 2 When Fees are Required

There are very specific times when a notary public must charge a fee:

In addition, notaries that are appointed to act for and on behalf of certain public agencies must charge for all services, but the fees collected must be remitted or turned over to the employing agency. (Government Code sections 6100 and 8202.5) The actual fee charged must be entered into the notary public's sequential journal. (Government Code section 8206(a))

Section 3 When Fees Cannot Be Charged

There are very specific times when a notary public is prohibited from charging a fee:

No fee shall be charged to notarize signatures on absentee ballot identification envelopes or other voting materials. (Government Code section 8211(d))

No notary public shall charge a fee for performing any official notarial duties on behalf of a veteran regarding service,

FAST FACTS:

No fee shall be charged to notarize signatures on absentee ballot identification envelopes or other voting materials (California Govern-ment Code 8211(d)).

discharge, separation, pension, insurance, compensation or any other veteran's benefit. (Government Code section 8211(f) and 6107)

No notary fee may be charged by notaries appointed to serve on military and naval reservations. (Government Code section 8203.6)

No notary public acting in his or her official capacity on behalf of the state, county, city or any other public body may charge to notarize an affidavit, application or voucher in relation to securing a pension. (Government Code section 6106)

No notary public shall charge a fee to notarize signatures on vote by mail ballot identification envelopes or other voting materials. (Government Code section 8211(d))

No notary public shall charge for notarizing any nomination document or circulator's affidavit. (California Elections Code section 8080)

Only notaries public employed by financial institutions, during the course and scope of the notary's employment with the financial institution, are authorized to demand acceptance and payment of foreign and inland bills of exchange or promissory notes or to protest for non-acceptance or nonpayment. (Government Code sections 8205 and 8208; Commercial Code section 3505)

The protest of a notary public acting in the course and scope of employment by a financial institution, under his or her hand and official seal, of a bill of exchange or promissory note for non-acceptance or nonpayment, specifying any of the following is prima facie evidence of the facts recited therein:

(a) The time and place of presentment.

(b) The fact that presentment was made and the manner thereof.

(c) The cause or reason for protesting the bill.

(d) The demand made and the answer given, if any, or the fact that the drawee or acceptor could not be found.

Section 4, Miscellaneous Fees

Travel fees: Although not mentioned in statue, The Notary Public Institute recommends that notaries public advise the constituent that the travel fees are separate from the notary fees. Additionally, we recommend that the fees are reasonable and agreed upon in advance

FAST FACTS:

Notarial fees may not be collected by notaries appointed to serve on military and naval reservations (California Govern-ment Code section 8203.6)

Chapter 5

TEST YOUR KNOWLEDGE

1) You must have errors and omissions insurance before you notarize any documents.
   a) True
   b) False

2) Errors and omission insurance protects the notary from the public.
   a) True
   b) False

3) A subscribing witness must see a principal signer affix his signature to a document.
   a) True
   b) False

4) The notary must personally know a subscribing witness.
   a) True
   b) False

5) Travel fees (although not mentioned in statute) must be reasonable and agreed to in advance.
   a) True
   b) False

6) The required bond for a California notary is $15,000.
   a) True
   b) False

7) A non-attorney notary may not charge more than $15.00 to complete a set of immigration forms.
   a) True
   b) False

8) A document that is incomplete may be notarized if the notary personally knows the signer.
   a) True
   b) False

9) A notary bond will protect the notary, up to the policy value, from honest mistakes.
   a) True
   b) False

10) Civil penalties for misconduct may include imprisonment.
    a) True
    b) False

Chapters 1 – 5

Test Your Knowledge Answers

Chapter 1

1. A   2.A   3.A   4.A   5.B   6.A   7.A   8.A   9.A   10.A

Chapter 2

1.A   2.A   3.A   4.B   5.B   6.A   7.A   8.B   9.A   10.A

Chapter 3

1.A   2.A   3.A   4.A   5.B   6.A   7.A   8.A   9.A   10.B

Chapter 4

1.B   2.A   3.A   4.B   5.A   6.A   7.A   8.A   9.A   10.A

Chapter 5

1.B   2.A   3.B   4.B   5.A   6.A   7.A   8.B   9.B   10.A

Chapter 6

Government Code

Civil Code

Code of Civil Procedure

Elections Code

Commercial Code

Probate Code

Penal Code

Business and Professions Code

8200. Appointment and commission; number; Jurisdiction

The Secretary of State may appoint and commission notaries public in such number, as the Secretary of State deems necess

ary for the public convenience. Notaries public may act as such notaries in any part of this state.

8201. Qulaifications to be a notary piblic: proof of course completion; reappointment

(a) Every person appointed as notary public shall meet all of the following requirements:

(1) Be at the time of appointment a legal resident of this state, except as otherwise provided in Section 8203.1.

(2) Be not less than 18 years of age.

(3) For appointments made on or after July 1, 2005, have satisfactorily completed a six-hour course of study approved by the Secretary of State pursuant to Section 8201.2 concerning the functions and duties of a notary public.

(4) Have satisfactorily completed a written examination prescribed by the Secretary of State to determine the fitness of the person to exercise the functions and duties of the office of notary public. All questions shall be based on the law of this state as set forth in the booklet of the laws of California relating to notaries public distributed by the Secretary of State.

(b) (1) Commencing July 1, 2005, each applicant for notary public shall provide satisfactory proof that he or she has completed the course of study required pursuant to paragraph (3) of subdivision (a) prior to approval of his or her appointment as a notary public by the Secretary of State.

(2) Commencing July 1, 2005, an applicant for notary public who holds a California notary public commission, and who has satisfactorily completed the six-hour course of study required pursuant to paragraph (1) at least one time, shall provide

satisfactory proof when applying for reappointment as a notary public that he or she has satisfactorily completed a three-hour refresher course of study prior to reappointment as a notary public by the Secretary of State.

8201.1. Additional qualifications; determination; identification; fingerprints

(a) Prior to granting an appointment as a notary public, the Secretary of State shall determine that the applicant possesses the required honesty, credibility, truthfulness, and integrity to fulfill the responsibilities of the position. To assist in determining the identity of the applicant and whether the applicant has been convicted of a disqualifying crime specified in subdivision (b) of Section 8214.1, the Secretary of State shall require that applicants be fingerprinted.

(b) Applicants shall submit to the Department of Justice fingerprint images and related information required by the department for the purpose of obtaining information as to the existence and content of a record of state and federal convictions and arrests and information as to the existence and content of a record of state and federal arrests for which the department establishes that the person is free on bail, or on his or her recognizance, pending trial or appeal.

(c) The department shall forward the fingerprint images and related information received pursuant to subdivision (a) to the Federal Bureau of Investigation and request a federal summary of criminal information.

(d) The department shall review the information returned from the Federal Bureau of Investigation and compile and disseminate a response to the Secretary of State pursuant to paragraph (1) of subdivision (p) of Section 11105 of the Penal Code.

(e) The Secretary of State shall request from the department subsequent arrest notification service, pursuant to Section 11105.2 of the Penal Code, for each person who submitted information pursuant to subdivision (a).

(f) The department shall charge a fee sufficient to cover the cost of processing the requests described in this section.

8201.2. Review of course of study for notary public; approval of education courase of study, violation of regulations; civil penalties

(a) The Secretary of State shall review the course of study proposed by any vendor to be offered pursuant to paragraph (3) of subdivision (a) and paragraph (2) of subdivision (b) of Section 8201. If the course of study includes all material that a person is expected to know to satisfactorily complete the written examination required pursuant to paragraph (4) of subdivision (a) of Section 8201, the Secretary of State shall approve the course of study.

(b) (1) The Secretary of State shall, by regulation, prescribe an application form and adopt a certificate of approval for the notary public education course of study proposed by a vendor.

(2) The Secretary of State may also provide a notary public education course of study.

(c) The Secretary of State shall compile a list of all persons offering an approved course of study pursuant to subdivision (a) and shall provide the list with every booklet of the laws of California relating to notaries public distributed by the Secretary of State.

(d) (1) A person who provides notary public education and violates any of the regulations adopted by the Secretary of State for approved vendors is subject to a civil penalty not to exceed one thousand dollars ($1,000) for each violation and shall be required to pay restitution where appropriate.

(2) The local district attorney, city attorney, or the Attorney General may bring a civil action to recover the civil penalty prescribed pursuant to this subdivision. A public prosecutor shall inform the Secretary of State of any civil penalty imposed under this section.

8201.5. Application form: confidential nature; use of information

The Secretary of State shall require an applicant for appointment and commission as a notary public to complete an application form and submit a photograph of their person as prescribed by the Secretary of State. Information on this form filed by an applicant with the Secretary of State, except for his or her name and address, is confidential and no individual record shall be divulged by an official or employee having access to it to any person other than the applicant, his or her authorized representative, or an employee or officer of the federal government, the state government, or a local agency, as defined in subdivision (b) of Section 6252 of the Government Code, acting in his or her official capacity. That information shall be used by the Secretary of State for the sole purpose of carrying out the duties of this chapter.

8202. Execution of jurat; administration of oath or affirmation to affiant; attachment to affidavit

(a) When executing a jurat, a notary shall administer an oath or affirmation to theaffiant and shall determine, from satisfactory evidence as described in Section1185 of the Civil Code, that the affiant is the person executing the document. The affiant shall sign the document in the presence of the notary.

(b) To any affidavit subscribed and sworn to before a notary, there shall be attached a jurat in the following form.

(The physical format of the boxed notice at the top of the jurat is required pursuant to subdivision (d) is an example, for purposes of illustration and not a limitation, of the physical format of a boxed notice fulfilling the requirements of subdivision (b)

(d) A jurat executed pursuant to this section shall be in the following form:

> A notary public or other officer completing this certificate verifies only the identity of the individual who signed the document to which this certificate is attached, and not the truthfulness, accuracy, or validity of that document.

State of California

County of _____

Subscribed and sworn to (or affirmed) before me on this _____ **day of** _____,

20___, by _____, **proved to me on the basis of satisfactory evidence to be the person(s) who appeared before me.**

Seal_____

Signature_____

8202.5. State, county and school district employees; certificates; expenses

The Secretary of State may appoint and commission the number of state, city, county, and public school district employees as notaries public to act for and on behalf of the governmental entity for which appointed which the Secretary of State deems proper. Whenever a notary is appointed and commissioned, a duly authorized representative of the employing governmental entity shall execute a certificate that the appointment is made for the purposes of the employing governmental entity, and whenever the certificate is filed with any state or county officer, no fees shall be charged by the officer for the filing or issuance of any document in connection with the appointment.

The state or any city, county, or school district for which the notary public is appointed and commissioned pursuant to this section may pay from any funds available for its support the premiums on any bond and the cost of any stamps, seals, or other supplies required in connection with the appointment, commission, or performance of the duties of the notary public.

Any fees collected or obtained by any notary public whose documents have been filed without charge and for whom bond premiums have been paid by the employer of the notary public shall be remitted by the notary public to the employing agency which shall deposit the funds to the credit of the fund from which the salary of the notary public is paid.

8202.7. Private employers; agreement to pay premium on bonds and cost of supplies; remission of fees to employer

A private employer, pursuant to an agreement with an employee who is a notary public, may pay the premiums on any bond and the cost of any stamps, seals, or other supplies required in connection with the appointment, commission, or performance of the duties of such notary public. Such agreement may also provide for the remission of fees collected by such notary public to the employer, in which case any fees collected or obtained by such notary public while such agreement is in effect shall be remitted by such notary public to the employer which shall deposit such funds to the credit of the fund from which the compensation of the notary public is paid.

8202.8. Private employers; limitation on provision of notorial services

Notwithstanding any other provision of law, a private employer of a notary public who has entered into an agreement with his or her employee pursuant to Section 8202.7 may limit, during the employee's ordinary course of employment, the providing of notarial services by the employee solely to transactions directly associated with the business purposes of the employer.

8203.1. Military and navel reservations, appointment and commission of notaries; qualifications

The Secretary of State may appoint and commission notaries public for the military and naval reservations of the Army, Navy, Coast Guard, Air Force, and Marine Corps of the United States, wherever located in the state; provided, however, that the appointee shall be a citizen of the United States, not less than 18 years of age, and must meet the requirements set forth in paragraphs (3) and (4) of subdivision (a) of Section 8201.

8203.2. Military and naval reservations, recommendation of commanding officer; jurisdiction of notary

Such notaries public shall be appointed only upon the recommendation of the commanding officer of the reservation in which they are to act, and they shall be authorized to act only within the boundaries of this reservation.

8203.3. Military and naval reservations; qualifications of notaries

In addition to the qualifications established in Section 8203.1, appointment will be made only from among those persons who are federal civil service employees at the reservation in which they will act as notaries public.

8203.4. Military and naval reservations; term of office; termination; resignation

The term of office shall be as set forth in Section 8204, except that the appointment shall terminate if the person shall cease to be employed as a federal civil service employee at the reservation for which appointed. The commanding officer of the reservation shall notify the Secretary of State of termination of employment at the reservation for which appointed within 30 days of such termination. A notary public whose appointment terminates pursuant to this section will have such termination treated as a resignation.

8203.5. Military and naval reservations, jurat

In addition to the name of the State, the jurat shall also contain the name of the reservation in which the instrument is executed.

8203.6. Military and naval reservations, fees

No fees shall be collected by such notaries public for service rendered within the reservation in the capacity of a notary public.

8204. Term of office

The term of office of a notary public is for four years commencing with the date specified in the commission.

8204.1. Cancellation of Commission ; failure to pay; notice

The Secretary of State may cancel the commission of a notary public if a check or other remittance accepted as payment for the examination, application, commission, and fingerprint fee is not paid upon presentation to the financial institution upon which the check or other remittance was drawn. Upon receiving written notification that the item presented for payment has not been honored for payment, the Secretary of State shall first give a written notice of the applicability of this section to the notary public or the person submitting the instrument. Thereafter, if the amount is not paid by a cashier's check or the equivalent, the Secretary of State shall give a second written notice of cancellation and the cancellation shall thereupon be effective. This second notice shall be given at least 20 days after the first notice, and no more than 90 days after the commencement date of the commission.

8205. Duties

(a) It is the duty of a notary public, when requested:

(1) To demand acceptance and payment of foreign and inland bills of exchange, or promissory notes, to protest them for nonacceptance and nonpayment, and, with regard only to the nonacceptance or nonpayment of bills and notes, to exercise any other powers and duties that by the law of nations and according to commercial usages, or by the laws of any other state, government, or country, may be performed by a notary. This paragraph applies only to a notary public employed by a financial institution, during the course and scope of the notary's

employment with the financial institution.

(2) To take the acknowledgment or proof of advance health care directives, powers of attorney, mortgages, deeds, grants, transfers, and other instruments of writing executed by any person, and to give a certificate of that proof or acknowledgment, endorsed on or attached to the instrument. The certificate shall be signed by the notary public in the notary public's own handwriting. A notary public may not accept any acknowledgment or proof of any instrument that is incomplete.

(3) To take depositions and affidavits, and administer oaths and affirmations, in all matters incident to the duties of the office, or to be used before any court, judge, officer, or board. Any deposition, affidavit, oath, or affirmation shall be signed by the notary public in the notary public's own handwriting.

(4) To certify copies of powers of attorney under Section 4307 of the Probate Code. The certification shall be signed by the notary public in the notary public's own handwriting.

(b) It shall further be the duty of a notary public, upon written request:

(1) To furnish to the Secretary of State certified copies of the notary's journal.

(2) To respond within 30 days of receiving written requests sent by certified mail from the Secretary of State's office for information relating to official acts performed by the notary.

8206. Sequential journal; contentsl thumbprint; loss of journal; copies of pages; exclusive property of notary public; limitations on surrender

(a) (1) A notary public shall keep one active sequential journal at a time, of all official acts performed as a notary public. The journal shall be kept in a locked and secured area, under the direct and exclusive control of the notary. Failure to secure the journal shall be cause for the Secretary of State to take administrative action against the commission held by the notary public pursuant to Section 8214.1.

(2) The journal shall be in addition to, and apart from, any copies of notarized documents that may be in the possession of the notary public and shall include all of the following:

(A) Date, time, and type of each official act.

(B) Character of every instrument sworn to, affirmed, acknowledged, or proved before the notary.

(C) The signature of each person whose signature is being notarized.

(D) A statement as to whether the identity of a person making an acknowledgment or taking an oath or affirmation was based on satisfactory evidence. If identity was established by satisfactory evidence pursuant to Section 1185 of the Civil Code, the journal shall contain the signature of the credible witness swearing or affirming to the identity of the individual or the type of identifying document, the governmental agency issuing the document, the serial or identifying number of the document, and the date of issue or expiration of the document.

(E) If the identity of the person making the acknowledgment or taking the oath or affirmation was established by the oaths or affirmations of two credible witnesses whose identities are proven to the notary public by presentation of any document satisfying the requirements of paragraph (3) or (4) of subdivision (b) of Section 1185 of the Civil Code, the notary public shall record in the journal the type of documents identifying the witnesses, the identifying numbers on the documents identifying the witnesses, and the dates of issuance or expiration of the documents identifying the witnesses.

(F) The fee charged for the notarial service.

(G) If the document to be notarized is a deed, quitclaim deed, deed of trust affecting real property, or a power of attorney document, the notary public shall require the party signing the document to place his or her right thumbprint in the journal. If the right thumbprint is not available, then the notary shall have the party use his or her left thumb, or any available finger and shall so indicate in the journal. If the party signing the document is physically unable to provide a thumbprint or fingerprint, the notary shall so indicate in the journal and shall also provide an explanation of that physical condition. This paragraph shall not apply to a trustee's deed resulting from a decree of foreclosure or a nonjudicial foreclosure pursuant to Section 2924 of the Civil Code, nor to a deed of reconveyance.

(b) If a sequential journal of official acts performed by a notary public is stolen, lost, misplaced, destroyed, damaged, or otherwise rendered unusable as a record of notarial acts and information, the notary public shall immediately notify the Secretary of State by certified or registered mail. The notification shall include the period of the journal entries, the notary public commission number, and the expiration date of the commission, and when applicable, a photocopy of any police report that specifies the theft of the sequential journal of official acts.

(c) Upon written request of any member of the public, which request shall include the name of the parties, the type of document, and the month and year in which notarized, the notary shall supply a photostatic copy of the line item representing the requested transaction at a cost of not more than thirty cents ($0.30) per page.

(d) The journal of notarial acts of a notary public is the exclusive property of that notary public, and shall not be surrendered to an employer upon termination of employment, whether or not the employer paid for the journal, or at any other time. The notary public shall not surrender the journal to any other person, except the county clerk, pursuant to Section 8209, or immediately, or if the journal is not present then as soon as possible, upon request to a peace officer investigating a criminal offense who has reasonable suspicion to believe the journal contains evidence of a criminal offense, as defined in Sections 830.1, 830.2, and 830.3 of the Penal Code, acting in his or her official capacity and within his or her authority. If the peace officer seizes the notary journal, he or she must have probable cause as required by the laws of this state and the United States. A peace officer or law enforcement agency that seizes a notary journal shall notify the Secretary of State by facsimile within 24 hours, or as soon as possible thereafter, of the name of the notary public whose journal has been seized. The notary public shall obtain a receipt for the journal, and shall notify the Secretary of State by certified mail within 10 days that the journal was relinquished to a peace officer. The notification shall include the period of the journal entries, the commission number of the notary public, the expiration date of the commission, and a photocopy of the receipt. The notary public shall obtain a new sequential journal. If the journal relinquished to a peace officer is returned to the notary public and a new journal has been obtained, the notary public shall make no new entries in the returned journal. A notary public who is an employee shall permit inspection and copying of journal transactions by a duly designated auditor or agent of the notary public's employer, provided that the inspection and copying is done in the presence of the notary public and the transactions are directly associated with the business purposes of the employer. The notary public, upon the request of the employer, shall regularly provide copies of all transactions that are directly associated with the business purposes of the employer, but shall not be required to provide copies of any transaction that is unrelated to the employer's business. Confidentiality and safekeeping of any copies of the journal provided to the employer shall be the responsibility of that employer.

(e) The notary public shall provide the journal for examination and copying in the presence of the notary public upon receipt of a subpoena duces tecum or a court order, and shall certify those copies if requested.

(f) Any applicable requirements of, or exceptions to, state and federal law shall apply to a peace officer engaged in the search or seizure of a sequential journal.

8206.5. Notaries; supplying photostatic copies on request; defending position in a discliplinary proceeding

Upon receiving a request for a copy of a transaction pursuant to subdivision (c) of Section 8206, the notary shall respond to the request within 15 business days after receipt of the request and either supply the photostatic copy requested or acknowledge that no such line item exists. In a disciplinary proceeding for noncompliance with subdivision (c) of Section 8206 or this section, a notary may defend his or her delayed action on the basis of unavoidable, exigent business or personal circumstances.

8207. Seal

A notary public shall provide and keep an official seal, which shall clearly show, when embossed, stamped, impressed or affixed to a document, the name of the notary, the State Seal, the words "Notary Public," and the name of the county wherein the bond and oath of office are filed, and the date the notary public's commission expires. The seal of every notary public commissioned on or after January 1, 1992, shall contain the sequential identification number assigned to the notary and the sequential identification number assigned to the manufacturer or vendor. The notary public shall authenticate with the official seal all official acts.

A notary public shall not use the official notarial seal except for the purpose of carrying out the duties and responsibilities as set forth in this chapter. A notary public shall not use the title "notary public" except for the purpose of rendering notarial service.

The seal of every notary public shall be affixed by a seal press or stamp that will print or emboss a seal, which legibly reproduces under photographic methods the required elements of the seal. The seal may be circular not over two inches in diameter, or may be a rectangular form of not more than one inch in width by two and one-half inches in length, with a serrated or milled edged border, and shall contain the information required by this section.

The seal shall be kept in a locked and secured area, under the direct and exclusive control of the notary. Failure to secure the seal shall be cause for the Secretary of State to take administrative action against the commission held by the notary public pursuant to Section 8214.1.

The official seal of a notary public is the exclusive property of that notary public, and shall not be surrendered to an employer upon the termination of employment, whether or not the employer paid for the seal, or to any other person. The notary, or his or her representative, shall destroy or deface the seal upon termination, resignation, or revocation of the notary's commission.

This section shall become operative on January 1, 1992.

8207.1. Identification number

The Secretary of State shall assign a sequential identification number to each notary which shall appear on the notary commission.

This section shall become operative on January 1, 1992.

8207.2. Manufacture, duplication, and sale of seal or stamp; procedures and guidelines for issuance of seals; certificate of authorization

(a) No notary seal or press stamp shall be manufactured, duplicated, sold, or offered for sale unless authorized by the Secretary of State.

(b) The Secretary of State shall develop and implement procedures and guidelines for the issuance of notary seals on or before January 1, 1992.

(c) The Secretary of State shall issue a permit with a sequential identification number to each manufacturer or vendor authorized to issue notary seals. The Secretary of State may establish a fee for the issuance of the permit which shall not exceed the actual costs of issuing the permit.

(d) The Secretary of State shall develop a certificate of authorization to purchase a notary stamp from an authorized vendor.

(e) The certificate of authorization shall be designed to prevent forgeries and shall contain a sequential identification number.

(f) This section shall become operative on January 1, 1992.

8207.3. Certificates of authorization; authorization to provide seal; lost; misplaced, damaged or therwise unworkable seal

(a) The Secretary of State shall issue certificates of authorization with which a notary public can obtain an official notary seal.

(b) A vendor or manufacturer is authorized to provide a notary with an official seal only upon presentation by the notary public of a certificate of authorization.

(c) A vendor of official seals shall note the receipt of certificates of authorization and sequential identification numbers of certificates presented by a notary public upon a certificate of authorization.

(d) A copy of a certificate of authorization shall be retained by a vendor and the original, which shall contain a sample impression of the seal issued to the notary public, shall be submitted to the Secretary of State for verification and recordkeeping. The Secretary of State shall develop guidelines for submitting certificates of authorization by vendors.

(e) Any notary whose official seal is lost, misplaced, destroyed, broken, damaged, or is rendered otherwise unworkable shall immediately mail or deliver written notice of that fact to the Secretary of State. The Secretary of State, within five working days after receipt of the notice, if requested by a notary, shall issue a certificate of authorization which a notary may use to obtain a replacement seal.

(f) This section shall become operative on January 1, 1992.

8207.4. Violations; penalties

(a) Any person who willfully violates any part of Section 8207.1, 8207.2, 8207.3, or 8207.4 shall be subject to a civil penalty not to exceed one thousand five hundred dollars ($1,500) for each violation, which may be recovered in a civil action brought by the Attorney General or the district attorney or city attorney, or by a city prosecutor in any city and county.

(b) The penalty provided by this section is not an exclusive remedy, and does not affect any other relief or remedy provided by law.

(c) This section shall become operative on January 1, 1992.

8208. Protest of bill or note for non-acceptance or nonpayment

The protest of a notary public acting in the course and scope of employment by a financial institution, under his or her hand and official seal, of a bill of exchange or promissory note for non-acceptance or nonpayment, specifying any of the following is prima facie evidence of the facts recited therein:

(a) The time and place of presentment.

(b) The fact that presentment was made and the manner thereof.

(c) The cause or reason for protesting the bill.

(d) The demand made and the answer given, if any, or the fact that the drawee or acceptor could not be found.

8209. Resignation, disqulaification or removal of notary; records delivered to clerk; misdemeanor;death; distruction of records

(a) If any notary public resigns, is disqualified, removed from office, or allows his or her appointment to expire without obtaining reappointment within 30 days, all notarial records and papers shall be delivered within 30 days to the clerk of the county in which the notary public's current official oath of office is on file. If the notary public willfully fails or refuses to deliver all notarial records and papers to the county clerk within 30 days, the person is guilty of a misdemeanor and shall be personally liable for damages to any person injured by that action or inaction.

(b) In the case of the death of a notary public, the personal representative of the deceased shall promptly notify the Secretary of State of the death of the notary public and shall deliver all notarial records and papers of the deceased to the clerk of the county in which the notary public's official oath of office is on file.

(c) After 10 years from the date of deposit with the county clerk, if no request for, or reference to such records has been made, they may be destroyed upon order of court.

8211. Fees

Fees charged by a notary public for the following services shall not exceed the fees prescribed by this section.

(a) For taking an acknowledgment or proof of a deed, or other instrument, to include the seal and the writing of the certificate, the sum of ten dollars ($15) for each signature taken.

(b) For administering an oath or affirmation to one person and executing the jurat, including the seal, the sum of ten dollars ($15).

(c) For all services rendered in connection with the taking of any deposition, the sum of twenty dollars ($30), and in addition thereto, the sum of five dollars ($7) for administering the oath to the witness and the sum of five dollars ($7) for the certificate to the deposition.

(d) No fee may be charged to notarize signatures on vote by mail ballot identification envelopes or other voting materials.

(e) For certifying a copy of a power of attorney under Section 4307 of the Probate Code the sum of ten dollars ($15).

(f) In accordance with Section 6107, no fee may be charged to a United States military veteran for notarization of an application or a claim for a pension, allotment, allowance, compensation, insurance, or any other veteran's benefit.

8212. Bond; amount; form

Every person appointed a notary public shall execute an official bond in the sum of fifteen thousand dollars ($15,000). The bond shall be in the form of a bond executed by an admitted surety insurer and not a deposit in lieu of bond.

8213. Bonds and oaths; filing; certificate; copy of oath as evidence; transfer to new county; name changes; fees

(a) No later than 30 days after the beginning of the term prescribed in the commission, every person appointed a notary public shall file an official bond and an oath of office in the office of the county clerk of the county within which the person maintains a principal place of business as shown in the application submitted to the Secretary of State, and the commission shall not take effect unless this is done within the 30-day period. A person appointed to be a notary public shall take and subscribe the oath of office either in the office of that county clerk or before another notary public in that county. If the oath of office is taken and subscribed before a notary public, the oath and bond may be filed with the county clerk by certified mail. Upon the filing of the oath and bond, the county clerk shall immediately transmit to the Secretary of State a certificate setting forth the fact of the filing and containing a copy of the official oath, personally signed by the notary public in the form set forth in the commission and shall immediately deliver the bond to the county recorder for recording. The county clerk shall retain the oath of office for one year following the expiration of the term of the commission for which the oath was taken, after which the oath may be destroyed or otherwise disposed of. The copy of the oath, personally signed by the notary public, on file with the Secretary of State may at any time be read in evidence with like effect as the original oath, without further proof.

(b) If a notary public transfers the principal place of business from one county to another, the notary public may file a new oath of office and bond, or a duplicate of the original bond with the county clerk to which the principal place of business was transferred. If the notary public elects to make a new filing, the notary public shall, within 30 days of the filing, obtain an official seal which shall include the name of the county to which the notary public has transferred. In a case where the notary public elects to make a new filing, the same filing and recording fees are applicable as in the case of the original filing and recording of the bond.

(c) If a notary public submits an application for a name change to the Secretary of State, the notary public shall, within 30 days from the date an amended commission is issued, file a new oath of office and an amendment to the bond with the county clerk in which the principal place of business is located. The amended commission with the name change shall not take effect unless the filing is completed within the 30-day period. The amended commission with the name change takes effect the date the oath and amendment to the bond is filed with the county clerk. If the principal place of business address was changed in the application for name change, either a new or duplicate of the original bond shall be filed with the county clerk with the amendment to the bond. The notary public shall, within 30 days of the filing, obtain an official seal that includes the name of the notary public and the name of the county to which the notary public has transferred, if applicable.

(d) The recording fee specified in Section 27361 of the Government Code shall be paid by the person appointed a notary public. The fee may be paid to the county clerk who shall transmit it to the county recorder.

(e) The county recorder shall record the bond and shall thereafter mail, unless specified to the contrary, it to the person named in the instrument and, if no person is named, to the party leaving it for recording.

8213.5. Change in location or address of business or residence notice

A notary public shall notify the Secretary of State by certified mail within 30 days as to any change in the location or address of the principal place of business or residence. A notary public shall not use a commercial mail receiving agency or post office box as his or her principal place of business or residence, unless the notary public also provides the Secretary of State with a physical street address as the principal place of residence. Willful failure to notify the Secretary of State of a change of address shall be punishable as an infraction by a fine of not more than five hundred dollars ($500).

8213.6. Name changes; application; filing

If a notary public changes his or her name, the notary public shall complete an application for name change form and file that application with the Secretary of State. Information on this form shall be subject to the confidentiality provisions described in Section 8201.5. Upon approval of the name change form, the Secretary of State shall issue a commission that reflects the new name of the notary public. The term of the commission and commission number shall remain the same. Willful failure to notify the Secretary of State of a name change shall be punishable as an infraction by a fine of not more than five hundred dollars ($500).

8214. Misconduct or neglect

For the official misconduct or neglect of a notary public, the notary public and the sureties on the notary public's official bond are liable in a civil action to the persons injured thereby for all the damages sustained.

8214.1. Grounds for refusal, revocation or suspension of commission

The Secretary of State may refuse to appoint any person as notary public or may revoke or suspend the commission of any notary public upon any of the following grounds:

(a) Substantial and material misstatement or omission in the application submitted to the Secretary of State to become a notary public.

(b) Conviction of a felony, a lesser offense involving moral turpitude, or a lesser offense of a nature incompatible with the duties of a notary public. A conviction after a plea of nolo contendere is deemed to be a conviction within the meaning of this subdivision.

(c) Revocation, suspension, restriction, or denial of a professional license, if the revocation, suspension, restriction, or denial was for misconduct based on dishonesty, or for any cause substantially relating to the duties or responsibilities of a notary public.

(d) Failure to discharge fully and faithfully any of the duties or responsibilities required of a notary public.

(e) When adjudicated liable for damages in any suit grounded in fraud, misrepresentation, or for a violation of the state regulatory laws, or in any suit based upon a failure to discharge fully and faithfully the duties as a notary public.

(f) The use of false or misleading advertising wherein the notary public has represented that the notary public has duties, rights, or privileges that he or she does not possess by law.

(g) The practice of law in violation of Section 6125 of the Business and Professions Code.

(h) Charging more than the fees prescribed by this chapter.

(i) Commission of any act involving dishonesty, fraud, or deceit with the intent to substantially benefit the notary public or another, or substantially injure another.

(j) Failure to complete the acknowledgment at the time the notary' s signature and seal are affixed to the document.

(k) Failure to administer the oath or affirmation as required by paragraph (3) of subdivision (a) of Section 8205.

(l) Execution of any certificate as a notary public containing a statement known to the notary public to be false.

(m) Violation of Section 8223.

(n) Failure to submit any remittance payable upon demand by the Secretary of State under this chapter or failure to satisfy any court-ordered money judgment, including restitution.

(o) Failure to secure the sequential journal of official acts, pursuant to Section 8206, or the official seal, pursuant to Section 8207, or willful failure to report the theft or loss of the sequential journal, pursuant to subdivision (b) of Section 8206.

(p) Violation of Section 8219.5.

(q) Commission of an act in violation of Section 6203, 8214.2, 8225, or 8227.3 of the Government Code or of Section 115, 470, 487, or 530.5 of the Penal Code.

(r) Willful failure to provide access to the sequential journal of official acts upon request by a peace officer.

8214.15. Civil Penalties

(a) In addition to any commissioning or disciplinary sanction, a violation of subdivision (f), (i), (l), (m), or (p) of Section 8214.1 is punishable by a civil penalty not to exceed one thousand five hundred dollars ($1,500).

(b) In addition to any commissioning or disciplinary sanction, a violation of subdivision (h), (j), or (k) of Section 8214.1, or a negligent violation of subdivision (d) of Section 8214.1 is punishable by a civil penalty not to exceed seven hundred fifty dollars ($750).

(c) The civil penalty may be imposed by the Secretary of State if a hearing is not requested pursuant to Section 8214.3. If a hearing is requested, the hearing officer shall make the determination.

(d) Any civil penalties collected pursuant to this section shall be transferred to the

General Fund. It is the intent of the Legislature that to the extent General Fund moneys are raised by penalties collected pursuant to this section, that money shall be made available to the Secretary of State's office to defray its costs of investigating and pursuing commissioning and monetary remedies for violations of the notary public law.

8214.2. Fraud relating to deed of trust; single-family residence; felony

(a) A notary public who knowingly and willfully with intent to defraud performs any notarial act in relation to a deed of trust on real property consisting of a single-family residence containing not more than four dwelling units, with knowledge that the deed of trust contains any false statements or is forged, in whole or in part, is guilty of a felony.

(b) The penalty provided by this section is not an exclusive remedy and does not affect any other relief or remedy provided by law.

8214.21. Failure to provide access to the sequential journal of notorial actsl civil penalties

A notary public who willfully fails to provide access to the sequential journal of notarial acts when requested by a peace officer shall be subject to a civil penalty not exceeding two thousand five hundred dollars ($2,500). An action to impose a civil penalty under this subdivision may be brought by the Secretary of State in an administrative proceeding or any public prosecutor in superior court, and shall be enforced as a civil judgment. A public prosecutor shall inform the secretary of any civil penalty imposed under this section.

8214.23. Failure to obtain thumbprint; civil penalties limitations

(a) A notary public who fails to obtain a thumbprint, as required by Section 8206, from a party signing a document shall be subject to a civil penalty not exceeding two thousand five hundred dollars ($2,500). An action to impose a civil penalty under this subdivision may be brought by the Secretary of State in an administrative proceeding or any public prosecutor in superior court, and shall be enforced as a civil judgment. A public prosecutor shall inform the secretary of any civil penalty imposed under this section.

(b) Notwithstanding any other limitation of time described in Section 802 of the Penal Code, or any other provision of law, prosecution for a violation of this offense shall be commenced within four years after discovery of the commission of the offense, or within four years after the completion of the offense, whichever is later.

8214.3. Hearing prior to denial or revocation of commission or imposition of civil penalities; law governing; expectations

Prior to a revocation or suspension pursuant to this chapter or after a denial of a commission, or prior to the imposition of a civil penalty, the person affected shall have a right to a hearing on the matter and the proceeding shall be conducted in accordance with Chapter 5 (commencing with Section 11500) of Part 1 of Division 3, except that a person shall not have a right to a hearing after a denial of an application for a notary public commission in either of the following cases:

(a) The Secretary of State has, within one year previous to the application, and after proceedings conducted in accordance with Chapter 5 (commencing with Section 11500) of Part 1 of Division 3, denied or revoked the applicant's application or commission.

(b) The Secretary of State has entered an order pursuant to Section 8214.4 finding that the applicant has committed or omitted acts constituting grounds for suspension or revocation of a notary public's commission.

8214.4. Resignation or expiration of commission not a bar or investigation or disciplinary proceedings

Notwithstanding this chapter or Chapter 5 (commencing with Section 11500) of Part 1 of Division 3, if the Secretary of State determines, after proceedings conducted in accordance with Chapter 5 (commencing with Section 11500) of Part 1 of Division 3, that any notary public has committed or omitted acts constituting grounds for suspension or revocation of a notary public's commission, the resignation or expiration of the notary public's commission shall not bar the Secretary of State from instituting or continuing an investigation or instituting disciplinary proceedings. Upon completion of the disciplinary proceedings, the Secretary of State shall enter an order finding the facts and stating the conclusion that the facts would or would not have constituted grounds for suspension or revocation of the commission if the commission had still been in effect.

8214.5. Revocation of commission; filing copy with county clerk

Whenever the Secretary of State revokes the commission of any notary public, the Secretary of State shall file with the county clerk of the county in which the notary public's principal place of business is located a copy of the revocation. The county clerk shall note such revocation and its date upon the original record of such certificate.

8214.8. Revocation upon certain convictions

Upon conviction of any offense in this chapter, or of Section 6203, or of any felony, of a person commissioned as a notary public, in addition to any other penalty, the court shall revoke the commission of the notary public, and shall require the notary public to surrender to the court the seal of the notary public. The court shall forward the seal, together with a certified copy of the judgment of conviction, to the Secretary of State.

8216. Release of Surety

When a surety of a notary desires to be released from responsibility on account of future acts, the release shall be pursuant to Article 11 (commencing with Section 996.110), and not by cancellation or withdrawal pursuant to Article 13 (commencing with Section 996.310), of Chapter 2 of Title 14 of Part 2 of the Code of Civil Procedure. For this purpose the surety shall make application to the superior court of the county in which the notary public's principal place of business is located and the copy of the application and notice of hearing shall be served on the Secretary of State as the beneficiary.

8219.5. Advertising in language other than English; posting of notice relating to legal advice and fees; translation of notary public into Spanish; suspension

(a) Every notary public who is not an attorney who advertises the services of a notary public in a language other than English by signs or other means of written communication, with the exception of a single desk plaque, shall post with that advertisement a notice in English and in the other language which sets forth the following:

(1) This statement: I am not an attorney and, therefore, cannot give legal advice about immigration or any other legal matters.

(2) The fees set by statute which a notary public may charge.

(b) The notice required by subdivision (a) shall be printed and posted as prescribed by the Secretary of State.

(c) Literal translation of the phrase "notary public" into Spanish, hereby defined as "notario publico" or "notario," is prohibited. For purposes of this subdivision, "literal translation" of a word or phrase from one language to another means the translation of a word or phrase without regard to the true meaning of the word or phrase in the language which is being translated.

(d) The Secretary of State shall suspend for a period of not less than one year or revoke the commission of any notary public who fails to comply with subdivision (a) or (c). However, on the second offense the commission of such notary public shall be revoked permanently.

8220. Rules and Regulations

The Secretary of State may adopt rules and regulations to carry out the provisions of this chapter.   The regulations shall be adopted in accordance with the Administrative Procedure Act (Chapter 3.5 (commencing with Section 11340) of Part 1 of Division 3).

8221. Destruction, defacement or concealment of records or papers; misdemeanor; liability for damages

(a) If any person shall knowingly destroy, deface, or conceal any records or papers belonging to the office of a notary public, such person shall be guilty of a misdemeanor and be liable in a civil action for damages to any person injured as a result of such destruction, defacing, or concealment.

(b) Notwithstanding any other limitation of time described in Section 802 of the Penal Code, or any other provision of law, prosecution for a violation of this offense shall be commenced within four years after discovery of the commission of the offense, or within four years after the completion of the offense, whichever is later.

(c) The penalty provided by this section is not an exclusive remedy and does not affect any other relief or remedy provided by law.

8222. Injunction; reimbursement for expenses

(a) Whenever it appears to the Secretary of State that any person has engaged or is about to engage in any acts or practices which constitute or will constitute a violation of any provision of this chapter or any rule or regulation prescribed under the authority thereof, the Secretary of State may apply for an injunction, and upon a proper showing, any court of competent jurisdiction has power to issue a permanent or temporary injunction or restraining order to enforce the provisions of this chapter, and any party to the action has the right to prosecute an appeal from the order or judgment of the court.

(b) The court may order a person subject to an injunction or restraining order provided for in this section to reimburse the Secretary of State for expenses incurred in the investigation related to the petition. The Secretary of State shall refund any amount received as reimbursement should the injunction or restraining order be dissolved by an appellate court.

8223. Notary public with expertise in immigration matters; advertising status as notary public; entry of information on forms; fees limitations

(a) No notary public who holds himself or herself out as being an immigration specialist, immigration consultant or any other title or description reflecting an expertise in immigration matters shall advertise in any manner whatsoever that he or she is a notary public.

(b) A notary public qualified and bonded as an immigration consultant under Chapter 19.5 (commencing with Section 22440) of Division 8 of the Business and Professions Code may enter data, provided by the client, on immigration forms provided by a federal or state agency. The fee for this service shall not exceed ten dollars ($10) per individual for each set of forms. If notary services are performed in relation to the set of immigration forms, additional fees may be collected pursuant to Section 8211. This fee limitation shall not apply to an attorney, who is also a notary public, who is rendering professional services regarding immigration matters.

(c) Nothing in this section shall be construed to exempt a notary public who enters data on an immigration form at the direction of a client, or otherwise performs the services of an immigration consultant, as defined by Section 22441 of the Business and Professions Code, from the requirements of Chapter 19.5 (commencing with Section 22440) of Division 8 of the Business and Professions Code. A notary public who is not qualified and bonded as an immigration consultant under Chapter 19.5 (commencing with Section 22440) of Division 8 of the Business and Professions Code may not enter data provided by a client on immigration forms nor otherwise perform the services of an immigration consultant.

8224. Conflict of interest; financial or beneficial interest in transaction; exceptions

A notary public who has a direct financial or beneficial interest in a transaction shall not perform any notarial act in connection with such transaction.   For purposes of this section, a notary public has a direct financial or beneficial interest in a transaction if the notary public:

(a) With respect to a financial transaction, is named, individually, as a principal to the transaction.

(b) With respect to real property, is named, individually, as a grantor, grantee, mortgagor, mortgagee, trustor, trustee, beneficiary, vendor, vendee, lessor, or lessee, to the transaction.   For purposes of this section, a notary public has no direct financial or beneficial interest in a transaction where the notary public acts in the capacity of an agent, employee, insurer, attorney, escrow, or lender for a person having a direct financial or beneficial interest in the transaction.

8224.1. Writings, depositions or affidavits of notary public; prohibitions against proof or taking by that notary public

A notary public shall not take the acknowledgment or proof of instruments of writing executed by the notary public nor shall depositions or affidavits of the notary public be taken by the notary public.

8225. Improper notorial acts, solicitation, coercion or influence of performance

(a) Any person who solicits, coerces, or in any manner influences a notary public to perform an improper notarial act knowing that act to be an improper notarial act, including any act required of a notary public under Section 8206, shall be guilty of a misdemeanor.

(b) Notwithstanding any other limitation of time described in Section 802 of the Penal Code, or any other provision of law, prosecution for a violation of this offense shall be commenced within four years after discovery of the commission of the offense, or within four years after the completion of the offense, whichever is later.

(c) The penalty provided by this section is not an exclusive remedy, and does not affect any other relief or remedy provided by law.

8227.1. Unlawful acts by one not a notary public; misdemeanor

It shall be a misdemeanor for any person who is not a duly commissioned, qualified, and acting notary public for the State of California to do any of the following:

(a) Represent or hold himself or herself out to the public or to any person as being entitled to act as a notary public.

(b) Assume, use or advertise the title of notary public in such a manner as to convey the impression that the person is a notary public.

(c) Purport to act as a notary public.

8227.3. Unlawful acts by one not a a notary public; deeds of trust on single-family residences; felony

Any person who is not a duly commissioned, qualified, and acting notary public who does any of the acts prohibited by Section 8227.1 in relation to any document or instrument affecting title to, placing an encumbrance on, or placing an interest secured by a mortgage or deed of trust on, real property consisting of a single-family residence containing not more than four dwelling units, is guilty of a felony.

8228. Enforcement of chapter; examination of notorial books, records, etc.

The Secretary of State or a peace officer, as defined in Sections 830.1, 830.2, and 830.3 of the Penal Code, possessing reasonable suspicion and acting in his or her official capacity and within his or her authority, may enforce the provisions of this chapter through the examination of a notary public's books, records, letters, contracts, and other pertinent documents relating to the official acts of the notary public.

8228.1. Willful failure to perform duty or control notorial seal

(a) Any notary public who willfully fails to perform any duty required of a notary public under Section 8206, or who willfully fails to keep the seal of the notary public under the direct and exclusive control of the notary public, or who surrenders the seal of the notary public to any person not otherwise authorized by law to possess the seal of the notary, shall be guilty of a misdemeanor.

(b) Notwithstanding any other limitation of time described in Section 802 of the Penal Code or any other provision of law, prosecution for a violation of this offense shall be commenced within four years after discovery of the commission of the offense, or within four years after the completion of the offense, whichever is later.

(c) The penalty provided by this section is not an exclusive remedy, and does not affect any other relief or remedy provided by law.

8230. Identification of affiant; verification

If a notary public executes a jurat and the statement sworn or subscribed to is contained in a document purporting to identify the affiant, and includes the birthdate or age of the person and a purported photograph or finger or thumbprint of the person so swearing or subscribing, the notary public shall require, as a condition to executing the jurat, that the person verify the birthdate or age contained in the statement by showing either:

(a) A certified copy of the person's birth certificate, or

(b) An identification card or driver's license issued by the Department of Motor Vehicles.

For the purposes of preparing for submission of forms required by the United States Immigration and Naturalization Service, and only for such purposes, a notary public may also accept for identification any documents or declarations acceptable to the United States Immigration and Naturalization Service.

§ 1360. Necessity of taking constitutional oath

Unless otherwise provided, before any officer enters on the duties of his office, he shall take and subscribe the oath or affirmation set forth in Section 3 of Article XX of the Constitution of California.

§ 1362. Administration by authorized officer

Unless otherwise provided, the oath may be taken before any officer authorized to administer oaths.

§ 6100. Performance of services; officers; notaries public

Officers of the state, or of a county or judicial district, shall not perform any official services unless upon the payment of the fees prescribed by law for the performance of the services, except as provided in this chapter.

This section shall not be construed to prohibit any notary public, except a notary public whose fees are required by law to be remitted to the state or any other public agency, from performing notarial services without charging a fee.

§ 6106. Pensions

Neither the State, nor any county or city, nor any public officer or body acting in his official capacity on behalf of the State, any county, or city, including notaries public, shall receive any fee or compensation for services rendered in an affidavit, or application relating to the securing of a pension, or the payment of a pension voucher, or any matter relating thereto.

§ 6107. Veterans

(a) No public entity, including the state, a county, city, or other political subdivision, nor any officer or employee thereof, including notaries public, shall demand or receive any fee or compensation for doing any of the following:

(1) Recording, indexing, or issuing certified copies of any discharge, certificate of service, certificate of satisfactory service, notice of separation, or report of separation of any member of the Armed Forces of the United States.

(2) Furnishing a certified copy of, or searching for, any public record that is to be used in an application or claim for a pension, allotment, allowance, compensation, insurance (including automatic insurance), or any other benefits under any act of Congress for service in the Armed Forces of the United States or under any law of this state relating to veterans' benefits.

(3) Furnishing a certified copy of, or searching for, any public record that is required by the Veterans Administration to be used in determining the eligibility of any person to participate in benefits made available by the Veterans Administration.

(4) Rendering any other service in connection with an application or claim referred to in paragraph (2) or (3).

(b) A certified copy of any record referred to in subdivision (a) may be made available only to one of the following:

(1) The person who is the subject of the record upon presentation of proper photo identification.

(2) A family member or legal representative of the person who is the subject of the record upon presentation of proper photo identification and certification of their relationship to the subject of the record.

(3) A county office that provides veteran's benefits services upon written request of that office.

(4) A United States official upon written request of that official. A public officer or employee is liable on his or her official bond for failure or refusal to render the services.

§ 6108. Oaths of office; claim against counties

No officer of a county or judicial district shall charge or receive any fee or compensation for administering or certifying the oath of office or for filing or swearing to any claim or demand against any county in the State.

§ 6109. Receipt of fees; written account; officer liability

Every officer of a county or judicial district, upon receiving any fees for official duty or service, may be required by the person paying the fees to make out in writing and to deliver to the person a particular account of the fees. The account shall specify for what the fees, respectively, accrued, and the officer shall receipt it. If the officer refuses or neglects to do so when required, he is liable to the person paying the fees in treble the amount so paid.

§ 6110. Performance of services following payment; officer liability

Upon payment of the fees required by law, the officer shall perform the services required. For every failure or refusal to do so, the officer is liable upon his official bond.

§ 6203. False certificate or writing by officer

(a) Every officer authorized by law to make or give any certificate or other writing is guilty of a misdemeanor if he or she makes and delivers as true any certificate or writing containing statements which he or she knows to be false.

(b) Notwithstanding any other limitation of time described in Section 802 of the Penal Code, or any other provision of law, prosecution for a violation of this offense shall be commenced within four years after discovery of the commission of the offense, or within four years after the completion of the offense, whichever is later.

(c) The penalty provided by this section is not an exclusive remedy, and does not affect any other relief or remedy provided by law.

§ 6800. Computation of time in which act is to be done

The time in which any act provided by law is to be done is computed by excluding the first day, and including the last, unless the last day is a holiday, and then it is also excluded.

§ 27287. Acknowledgment of execution or proof by subscribing witness required before recording; exceptions

* * * before an instrument can be recorded its execution shall be acknowledged by the person executing it, or if executed by a corporation, by its president or secretary or other person executing it on behalf of the corporation, or, except for any power of attorney, quitclaim deed, or grant deed other than a trustee's deed or a deed of reconveyance, mortgage, deed of trust, or security agreement, proved by subscribing witness or as provided in Sections 1198 and 1199 of the Civil Code, and the acknowledgment or proof certified as prescribed by law.

§ 66433. Content and form; application of article

The content and form of final maps shall be governed by the provisions of this article.

§ 66436. Statement of consent; necessity; exceptions; nonliability for omission of signature; notary acknowledgment

(a) A statement, signed and acknowledged by all parties having any record title interest in the subdivided real property, consenting to the preparation and recordation of the final map is required, * * *

(c) A notary acknowledgment shall be deemed complete for recording without the official seal of the notary, so long as the name of the notary, the county of the notary's principal place of business, and the notary's commission expiration date are typed or printed below or immediately adjacent to the notary's signature in the acknowledgment.

(2) The oath or affirmation under penalty of perjury of two credible witnesses, whose identities are proven to the officer upon the presentation of any document satisfying the requirements of paragraph (3) or (4), that each statement in paragraph (1) is true.

(3) Reasonable reliance on the presentation to the officer of any one of the following, if the document is current or has been issued within five years:

(A) An identification card or driver's license issued by the Department of Motor Vehicles.

(B) A passport issued by the Department of State of the United States.

(4) Reasonable reliance on the presentation of any one of the following, provided that a document specified in subparagraphs (A) to (F), inclusive, shall either be current or have been issued within five years and shall contain a photograph and description of the person named on it, shall be signed by the person, shall bear a serial or other identifying number, and, in the event that the document is a passport, shall have been stamped by the United States Citizenship and Immigration Services of the Department of Homeland Security:

(A) A passport issued by a foreign government.

(B) A driver's license issued by a state other than California or by a Canadian or Mexican public agency authorized to issue driver's licenses.

(C) An identification card issued by a state other than California.

(D) An identification card issued by any branch of the Armed Forces of the United States.

(E) An inmate identification card issued on or after January 1, 1988, by the Department of Corrections and Rehabilitation, if the inmate is in custody.

(F) An employee identification card issued by an agency or office of the State of California, or by an agency or office of a city, county, or city and county in this state.

(G) An inmate identification card issued prior to January 1, 1988, by the Department of Corrections and Rehabilitation, if the inmate is in custody.

(c) An officer who has taken an acknowledgment pursuant to this section shall be presumed to have operated in accordance with the provisions of law.

(d) A party who files an action for damages based on the failure of the officer to establish the proper identity of the person making the acknowledgment shall have the burden of proof in establishing the negligence or misconduct of the officer.

(e) A person convicted of perjury under this section shall forfeit any financial interest in the document.

§ 1188. Certificate of acknowledgment

An officer taking the acknowledgment of an instrument shall endorse thereon or attach thereto a certificate in the form prescribed in California Civil Code section **§ 1189. Certificate of acknowledgment; form; sufficiency of out of state**

acknowledgment; force and effect of acknowledgment under prior laws

(a)(1) Any certificate of acknowledgment taken within this state shall be in the

following form:

> A notary public or other officer completing this certificate verifies only the identity of the individual who signed the document to which this certificate is attached, and not the truthfulness, accuracy, or validity of that document.

State of California }

County of _____

On _____ before me, (here insert name and title of the officer), personally

appeared

_____

_____

_____

_____ _____, who proved to me on the basis of satisfactory evidence to be the person(s) whose name(s) is/are subscribed to the within instrument and acknowledged to me that he/she/they executed the same in his/her/their authorized capacity(ies), and that by his/her/their signature(s) on the instrument the person(s), or the entity upon behalf of which the person(s) acted, executed the instrument.
I certify under PENALTY OF PERJURY under the laws of the State of California

that the foregoing paragraph is true and correct.

WITNESS my hand and official seal.

Signature _____ (Seal)

(2) A notary public who willfully states as true any material fact that he or she knows to be false shall be subject to a civil penalty not exceeding ten thousand dollars ($10,000). An action to impose a civil penalty under this subdivision may be brought by the Secretary of State in an administrative proceeding or any public prosecutor in superior court, and shall be enforced as a civil judgment. A public prosecutor shall inform the secretary of any civil penalty imposed under this section.

(b) Any certificate of acknowledgment taken in another place shall be sufficient in this state if it is taken in accordance with the laws of the place where the acknowledgment is made.

(c) On documents to be filed in another state or jurisdiction of the United States, a California notary public may complete any acknowledgment form as may be required in that other state or jurisdiction on a document, provided the form does not require the notary to determine or certify that the signer holds a particular representative capacity or to make other determinations and certifications not allowed by California law.

(d) An acknowledgment provided prior to January 1, 1993, and conforming to applicable provisions of former Sections 1189, 1190, 1190a, 1190.1, 1191, and 1192, as repealed by Chapter 335 of the Statutes of 1990, shall have the same force and effect as if those sections had not been repealed.

§ 1190. Certificate of acknowledgment as prima facie evidence; duly authorized person

The certificate of acknowledgment of an instrument executed on behalf of an incorporated or unincorporated entity by a duly authorized person in the form specified in Section 1189 shall be prima facie evidence that the instrument is the duly authorized act of the entity named in the instrument and shall be conclusive evidence thereof in favor of any good faith purchaser, lessee, or encumbrancer. "Duly authorized person," with respect to a domestic or foreign corporation, includes the president, vice president, secretary, and assistant secretary of the corporation.

§ 1193. Certificate of acknowledgment; authentication

Officers taking and certifying acknowledgments or proof of instruments for record, must authenticate their certificates by affixing thereto their signatures, followed by the names of their offices; also, their seals of office, if by the laws of the State or country where the acknowledgment or proof is taken, or by authority of which they are acting, they are required to have official seals.43 civil code

§ 1195. Proof of execution; methods; certificate form

(a) Proof of the execution of an instrument, when not acknowledged, may be made by any of the following:

(1) By the party executing it, or either of them.

(2) By a subscribing witness.

(3) By other witnesses, in cases mentioned in Section 1198.

(b) (1) Proof of the execution of a power of attorney, grant deed, mortgage, deed of trust, quitclaim deed, or security agreement is not permitted pursuant to Section 27287 of the Government Code, though proof of the execution of a trustee's deed or deed of reconveyance is permitted.

(2) Proof of the execution for any instrument requiring a notary public to obtain a thumbprint from the party signing the document in the notary public's journal is not permitted.

(c) Any certificate for proof of execution taken within this state must be in the following form:

> A notary public or other officer completing this certificate verifies only the identity of the individual who signed the document to which this certificate is attached, and not the truthfulness, accuracy, or validity of that document.

State of California } ss.

County of _____

On _____ (date), before me, _____ (name and title of officer), personally appeared_____ (name of subscribing witness), proved to me to be the person whose name is subscribed to the within instrument, as a witness thereto, on the oath of _____ (name of credible witness), a credible witness who is known to me and provided a satisfactory identifying document. _____(name of subscribing witness), being by me duly sworn, said that he/she was present and saw/heard _____ (name[s] of principal[s]), the same person(s) described in and whose name(s) is/are subscribed to the within or attached instrument in his/her/their authorized capacity(ies) as (a) party(ies) thereto, execute or acknowledge executing the same, and that said affiant subscribed his/her name to the within or attached instrument as a witness at the request of _____ (name[s] of principal[s]).

WITNESS my hand and official seal.

Signature _____ (Seal)

BUSINESS AND PROFESSIONS CODE

22449. Deferred Action for Childhood Arrivals program; price gouging; penalties

(a)   Immigration consultants, attorneys, notaries public, and organizations accredited by the United States Board of Immigration Appeals shall be the only individuals authorized to charge clients or prospective clients fee for providing consultations, legal advise, or notary public services respectively, associated with filing an application under the federal Deferred Action for Childhood Arrivals program announced by the United States Secretary of Homeland Security on June 15, 2012.

(b)   (1) Immigration consultants, attorneys, notaries public, and organizations accredited by the United States Board of Immigration Appeals shall be prohibited from participating in practices that that amount to price gouging when a client or prospective client solicits services associates with filing an application for deferred action for childhood arrivals as described in subdivision (a).

(2)   For the purposes of this section, "price gouging" means any practice that has the effect of pressuring the client or prospective client to purchase services immediately because purchasing them at a later time will result in the client or prospective client paying a higher price for the same services.

(c) (1) In addition to civil and criminal penalties described in Section 22445, a violation of this section by an attorney shall be cause for discipline by the State Bar pursuant to chapter 4 (commencing with Section 6000) of Division 3.

(2) In addition to civil and criminal penalties described in Section 22445, a violation of this section by a notary public shall be cause for revocation or suspension of his or her commission as a notary public by the Secretary of State and the application of any other applicable penalties pursuant to Chapter 3 (commencing with Section 8200) of Division 1 of Title 2 of the Government Code.

§ 1196. Subscribing witness; establishment of identity

A witness shall be proved to be a subscribing witness by the oath of a credible witness who provides the officer with any document satisfying the requirements of paragraph (3) or (4) of subdivision (b) of Section 1185.

§ 1197. Subscribing witness; items to be proved

The subscribing witness must prove that the person whose name is subscribed to the instrument as a party is the person described in it, and that such person executed it, and that the witness subscribed his name thereto as a witness.

§ 1633.11. Notarization and signature under penalty of perjury requirements

(a) If a law requires that a signature be notarized, the requirement is satisfied with respect to an electronic signature if an electronic record includes, in addition to the electronic signature to be notarized, the electronic signature of a notary public together with all other information required to be included in a notarization by other applicable law.

§ 1633.12. Retaining records; electronic satisfaction

(a) If a law requires that a record be retained, the requirement is satisfied by retaining an electronic record of the information in the record, if the electronic record reflects accurately the information set forth in the record at the time it was first generated in its final form as an electronic record or otherwise, and the electronic record remains accessible for later reference.

(b) A requirement to retain a record in accordance with subdivision (a) does not apply to any information the sole purpose of which is to enable the record to be sent, communicated, or received.

(c) A person may satisfy subdivision (a) by using the services of another person if the requirements of subdivision (a) are satisfied.

(d) If a law requires a record to be retained in its original form, or provides consequences if the record is not retained in its original form, that law is satisfied by an electronic record retained in accordance with subdivision (a).

(e) If a law requires retention of a check, that requirement is satisfied by retention of an electronic record of the information on the front and back of the check in accordance with subdivision (a).

(f) A record retained as an electronic record in accordance with subdivision (a) satisfies a law requiring a person to retain a record for evidentiary, audit, or like purposes, unless a law enacted after the effective date of this title specifically prohibits the use of an electronic record for a specified purpose.

(g) This section does not preclude a governmental agency from specifying additional requirements for the retention of a record subject to the agency's jurisdiction.

CODE OF CIVIL PROCEDURE

§ 12a. Computation of time; holidays; application of section

(a) If the last day for the performance of any act provided or required by law to be performed within a specified period of time is a holiday, then that period is hereby extended to and including the next day that is not a holiday. For purposes of this section, "holiday" means all day on Saturdays, all holidays specified in Section 135 and, to the extent provided in Section 12b, all days that by terms of Section 12b are required to be considered as holidays.

§ 1935. Subscribing witness defined

A subscribing witness is one who sees a writing executed or hears it acknowledged, and at the request of the party thereupon signs his name as a witness.

§ 2093. Officers authorized to administer oaths or affirmations

(a) Every court, every judge, or clerk of any court, every justice, and every notary public, and every officer or person authorized to take testimony in any action or proceeding, or to decide upon evidence, has the power to administer oaths or affirmations.

(b) (1) Every shorthand reporter certified pursuant to Article 3 (commencing with Section 8020) of Chapter 13 of Division 3 of the Business and Professions Code has the power to administer oaths or affirmations and may perform the duties of the deposition officer pursuant to Chapter 9 (commencing with Section 2025.010) of Title 4. The certified shorthand reporter shall be entitled to receive fees for services rendered during a deposition, including fees for deposition services, as specified in subdivision (c) of Section 8211 of the Government Code.

(2) This subdivision shall also apply to depositions taken by telephone or other remote electronic means as specified in Chapter 2 (commencing with Section 2017.010), Chapter 3 (commencing with Section 2017.710), and Chapter 9 (commencing with Section 2025.010) of Title 4.

(c) A former judge or justice of a court of record in this state who retired or resigned from office, other than a judge or justice who was retired by the Supreme Court for disability, shall have the power to administer oaths or affirmations, if the former judge or justice requests and receives a certification from the Commission on Judicial Performance that there was no formal disciplinary proceeding pending at the time of retirement or resignation. Where no formal disciplinary proceeding was pending at the time of retirement or resignation, the Commission on Judicial Performance shall issue the certification.

No law, rule, or regulation regarding the confidentiality of proceedings of the Commission on Judicial Performance shall be construed to prohibit the Commission on Judicial Performance from issuing a certificate as provided for in this section.

§ 2094.Oath to witness; form

(a) An oath, affirmation, or declaration in an action or a proceeding, may be administered by obtaining an affirmative response to one of the following questions:

(1) "Do you solemnly state that the evidence you shall give in this issue (or matter) shall be the truth, the whole truth, and nothing but the truth, so help you God?"

(2) "Do you solemnly state, under penalty of perjury, that the evidence that you shall give in this issue (or matter) shall be the truth, the whole truth, and nothing but the truth?"

ELECTIONS CODE

§ 8080. Fee for verification

No fee or charge shall be made or collected by any officer for verifying any nomination document or circulator's affidavit.

COMMERCIAL CODE

§ 3505. Protest; Noting for Protest

(b) A protest is a certificate of dishonor made by a United States consul or vice consul, or a notary public during the course and scope of employment with a financial institution or other person authorized to administer oaths by the laws of any other state, government, or country in the place where dishonor occurs. It may be made upon information satisfactory to that person. The protest shall identify the instrument and certify either that presentment has been made or, if not made, the reason why it was not made, and that the instrument has been dishonored by non-acceptance or nonpayment. The protest may also certify that notice of dishonor has been given to some or all parties.

PROBATE CODE

§ 4307. Certified copies of power of attorney

(a) A copy of a power of attorney certified under this section has the same force and effect as the original power of attorney.

(b) A copy of a power of attorney may be certified by any of the following:

(1) An attorney authorized to practice law in this state.

(2) A notary public in this state.

(3) An official of a state or of a political subdivision who is authorized to make certifications.

(c) The certification shall state that the certifying person has examined the original power of attorney and the copy and that the copy is a true and correct copy of the original power of attorney.

(d) Nothing in this section is intended to create an implication that a third person may be liable for acting in good faith reliance on a copy of a power of attorney that has not been certified under this section.

PENAL CODE

§ 17. Felony; misdemeanor; infraction; classification of offenses

(a) A felony is a crime that is punishable with death, by imprisonment in the state prison, or notwithstanding any other provision of law, by imprisonment in a county jail for more than one year. Every other crime or public offense is a misdemeanor except those offenses that are classified as infractions.***

§ 115.5.Filing false or forged documents relating to single-family residences; punishment; false statement to notary public

(a) Every person who files any false or forged document or instrument with the county recorder which affects title to, places an encumbrance on, or places an interest secured by a mortgage or deed of trust on, real property consisting of a single-family residence containing not more than four dwelling units, with knowledge that the document is false or forged, is punishable, in addition to any other punishment, by a fine not exceeding seventy-five thousand dollars ($75,000).

(b) Every person who makes a false sworn statement to a notary public, with knowledge that the statement is false, to induce the notary public to perform an improper notarial act on an instrument or document affecting title to, or placing an encumbrance on, real property consisting of a single-family residence containing not more than four dwelling units is guilty of a felony.

§ 118.Perjury defined; evidence necessary to support conviction

(a) Every person who, having taken an oath that he or she will testify, declare, depose, or certify truly before any competent tribunal, officer, or person, in any of the cases in which the oath may by law of the State of California be administered, willfully and contrary to the oath, states as true any material matter which he or she knows to be false, and every person who testifies, declares, deposes, or certifies under penalty of perjury in any of the cases in which the testimony, declarations, depositions, or certification is permitted by law of the State of California under penalty of perjury and willfully states as true any material matter which he or she knows to be false, is guilty of perjury.

This subdivision is applicable whether the statement, or the testimony, declaration, deposition, or certification is made or subscribed within or without the State of California.

(b) No person shall be convicted of perjury where proof of falsity rests solely upon contradiction by testimony of a single person other than the defendant. Proof of falsity may be established by direct or indirect evidence.

§ 126.Punishment

Perjury is punishable by imprisonment pursuant to subdivision (h) of Section 1170 for two, three or four years.

§ 470.Forgery; signatures or seals; corruption of records

(b) Every person who, with the intent to defraud, counterfeits or forges the seal or handwriting of another is guilty of forgery.

(d) Every person who, with the intent to defraud, falsely makes, alters, forges, or counterfeits, utters, publishes, passes or attempts or offers to pass, as true and genuine, any of the following items, knowing the same to be false, altered, forged, or counterfeited, is guilty of forgery: ... or falsifies the acknowledgment of any notary public, or any notary public who issues an acknowledgment knowing it to be false; or any matter described in subdivision (b).

§ 473.Forgery; punishment

Forgery is punishable by imprisonment in a county jail for not more than one year, or by imprisonment pursuant to subdivision (h) of Section 1170.

§ 830.3.Peace officers; employing agencies; authority

The following persons are peace officers whose authority extends to any place in the state for the purpose of performing their primary duty or when making an arrest pursuant to Section 836 as to any public offense with respect to which there is immediate danger to person or property, or of the escape of the perpetrator of that offense, or pursuant to Section 8597 or 8598 of the Government Code.***

(o) Investigators of the office of the Secretary of State designated by the Secretary of State, provided that the primary duty of these peace officers shall be the enforcement of the law as prescribed in Chapter 3 (commencing with Section 8200) of Division 1 of Title 2 of, and Section12172.5 of, the Government Code.***

CIVIL CODE

§ 14. Words and phrases; construction; tense; gender; number

Signature or subscription includes mark, when the person cannot write, his name being written near it, by a person who writes his own name as a witness; provided, that when a signature is by mark it must in order that the same may be acknowledged or may serve as the signature to any sworn statement be witnessed by two persons who must subscribe their own names as witnesses thereto.

§ 1181.Notaries public; officers before whom proof or acknowledgment may be made

The proof or acknowledgment of an instrument may be made before a notary public at any place within this state, or within the county or city and county in this state in which the officer specified below was elected or appointed, before either:

(a) A clerk of a superior court.

(b) A county clerk.

(c) A court commissioner.

(d) A retired judge of a municipal or justice court.

(e) A district attorney.

(f) A clerk of a board of supervisors.

(g) A city clerk.

(h) A county counsel.

(i) A city attorney.

(j) Secretary of the Senate.

(k) Chief Clerk of the Assembly.

§ 1185.Acknowledgments; requisites

(a) The acknowledgment of an instrument shall not be taken unless the officer taking it has satisfactory evidence that the person making the acknowledgment is the individual who is described in and who executed the instrument.

(b) For the purposes of this section "satisfactory evidence" means the absence of information, evidence, or other circumstances that would lead a reasonable person to believe that the person making the acknowledgment is not the individual he or she claims to be and any one of the following:

(1)(A) The oath or affirmation of a credible witness personally known to the officer, whose identity is proven to the officer upon presentation of a document satisfying the requirements of paragraph (3) or (4), that the person making the acknowledgment is personally known to the witness and that each of the following are true:

(i) The person making the acknowledgment is the person named in the document.

(ii) The person making the acknowledgment is personally known to the witness.

(iii) That it is the reasonable belief of the witness that the circumstances of the person making the acknowledgment are such that it would be very difficult or impossible for that person to obtain another form of identification.

(iv) The person making the acknowledgment does not possess any of the identification documents named in paragraphs (3) and (4).

(v) The witness does not have a financial interest in the document being acknowledged and is not named in the document.

(B) A notary public who violates this section by failing to obtain the satisfactory evidence required by subparagraph (A) shall be subject to a civil penalty not exceeding ten thousand dollars ($10,000). An action to impose this civil penalty may be brought by the Secretary of State in an administrative proceeding or a public prosecutor in superior court, and shall be enforced as a civil judgment. A public prosecutor shall inform the secretary of any civil penalty imposed under this subparagraph.

FEE SCHEDULE
Notary Fees

Notaries who charge for their service will find the maximum fees allowed to be charged in Government Code section §8211. The notary public may charge up to the maximum fees listed, but must not charge more, to do so could result in a fine, suspension, or revocation of the notary's commission. The notary public must keep track of all fees collected by making an entry in his or her notarial journal.

Travel Fees

When a notary public is asked to travel to meet with a constituent (outside of his or her office or normal place of business) to perform a notarial act, the notary public may charge a travel fee, which is separate from the normal notarial fee. The Notary Public Institute recommends that travel fees are resonable and agreed upon in advance. Additionally, the constituent must be made aware (in advance) that he or she is being charged a separate travel fee for the transaction.

Fee Schedule
(Government Code section 8211 and 8206)

Acknowledgment	**$15.00**
Jurat	**$15.00**
Deposition *(Plus $7.00 for certificate)*	**$30.00**
Oath to the Witness *(administered for a deposition)*	**$7.00**
Certificate to the Deposition	**$7.00**
Protest for Non-Payment	**$0.00**
Serving Notice of Non-Payment	**$0.00**
Recording Every Protest	**$0.00**
Circulator's Affidavit [Nomination]	**$0.00**
Certifying Copy of Line Item in the Journal	**$0.30**
Certifying Power of Attorney	**$15.00**
Vote by Mail	**$0.00**

ABIDE - To accept the consequences of.

ABJURE - To renounce; give up.

ABRIDGE - To reduce; contract; diminish.

ABROGATE - To annul, repeal, or destroy.

ABSCOND - To hide or absent oneself to avoid legal action.

ABSTRACT - A summary.

ABUT - To border on, to touch.

ACCESS - Approach; in real property law it means the right of the owner of property to the use of the highway or road next to his land, without obstruction by intervening property owners.

ACCESSORY - In criminal law, it means the person who contributes or aids in the commission of a crime.

ACCOMPLICE - In criminal law, it means a person who together with the principal offender commits a crime.

ACCORD - An agreement to accept something different or less than that to which one is entitled, which extinguishes the entire obligation.

ACCOUNT - A statement of mutual demands in the nature of debt and credit between parties.

ACCRUE - To grow to be added to.

ACKNOWLEDGMENT - The act of going before an official authorized to take acknowledgments. A notary certifies having positively identified a document signer who personally appeared before the notary. *In an effort to help reduce fraud, The Notary Public Institute recommends that the notary confirm that the constituent acknowledges signing the document of his or her own free will.*

ACQUIESCENCE - A silent appearance of consent.

ACQUIT - To legally determine the innocence of one charged with a crime.

ACTION - "Action" includes a civil action and a criminal action.

ADJECTIVE LAW - Rules of procedure.

ADJUDICATION - The judgment given in a case.

ADMINISTRATOR – To give formally, as in giving an oath or affirmation.

ADULT - Sixteen years old or over (in criminal law).

ADVERSE - Opposed; contrary.

ADVOCATE - (v) To speak in favor of; (n.) One who assists, defends, or pleads for another.

AFFIANT - A person who makes and signs an affidavit.

AFFIDAVIT - A written and sworn to declaration of facts, voluntarily made.

AFFINITY - The relationship between persons through marriage with the kindred of each other; distinguished from consanguinity, which is the relationship by blood.

AFFIRM - To ratify; also when an appellate court affirms a judgment, decree, or order, it means that it is valid and right and must stand as rendered in the lower court.

AFOREMENTIONED; AFORESAID - Before or already said.

AGENT - One who represents and acts for another.

AKA – Abbreviation for "also known as".

ALIAS - A name not one's true name.

ALIBI - A claim of not being present at a certain place at a certain time.

ALLEGE - To assert.

ALTERATION – Creating a false document by changing or altering its content.

AMBIGUITY - Uncertainty; capable of being understood in more than one way.

AMENDMENT - Any language made or proposed as a change in some principal writing.

ANCILLARY - Aiding, auxiliary.

ANNOTATION - A note added by way of comment or explanation.

ANSWER – A written statement made by a defendant setting forth the grounds of his defense.

ANTE - Before.

APPEAL - The removal of a case from a lower court to one of superior jurisdiction for the purpose of obtaining a review.

APPEARANCE - Coming into court as a party to a suit.

APPELLANT - The party who takes an appeal from one court or jurisdiction to another (appellate) court for review.

APPELLEE - The party against whom an appeal is taken.

APPURTENANT - Belonging to; accessory or incident to.

ARBITER - One who decides a dispute; a referee.

ARBITRARY - Unreasoned; not governed by any fixed rules or standard.

ARGUENDO - By way of argument.

ASSENT - A declaration of willingness to do something in compliance with a request.

ASSERT - Declare.

ASSESS -To fix the rate or amount.

ASSIGN - To transfer; to appoint; to select for a particular purpose.

ASSIGNEE - One who receives an assignment.

ASSIGNOR - One who makes an assignment.

AT ISSUE - When parties in an action come to a point where one asserts something and the other denies it.

ATTACH - Seize property by court order and sometimes arrest a person.

ATTEST - To witness a will, etc.; act of attestation.

ATTESTATION - To indicate genuineness by signing as a witness

ATTESTIONATION – To sign as a witness. An act of confirming officially.

ATTORNEY-IN FACT – Individual that has authority to sign for another.

AVERMENT - A positive statement of facts.

AWARENESS – Being able to understand the significance of a document.

BAIL - To obtain the release of a person from legal-custody by giving security and promising that he shall appear in court; to deliver (goods, etc.) in trust to a person for a special purpose.

BAILEE - One to whom personal property is delivered under a contract of bailment.

BAILMENT - Delivery of personal property to another to be held for a certain purpose and to be returned when the purpose is accomplished.

BANKRUPT - An insolvent enterprise or person, technically, one declared to be bankrupt after a bankruptcy proceeding.

BAR - The legal profession.

BARTER - A contract by which parties exchange goods for other goods.

BENEFICIARY - A person benefiting under a will, trust, or agreement.

BEQUEST - A gift of personal property under a will.

BONA FIDE - In or with good faith; honestly.

BOND - An instrument by which the maker promises to pay a sum of money to another, usually providing that upon performances of a certain condition the obligation shall be void.

BREACH - The breaking or violating of a law, or the failure to carry out a duty.

BRIEF - A written document, prepared by a lawyer to serve as the basis of an argument upon a case in court, usually an appellate court.

BUSINESS - Shall include every kind of business, profession, occupation, calling or operation of institutions, whether carried on for profit or not.

BY-LAWS - Regulations, ordinances, or rules enacted by a corporation, association, etc., for its own government.

C

CANON - A doctrine; also, a law or rule, of a church or association in particular.

CAPTION - In a pleading, deposition or other paper connected with a case in court, it is the heading or introductory clause which shows the names of the parties, name of the court, number of the case on the docket or calendar, etc.

CASE - A general term for an action, cause, suit, or controversy before a judicial body.

CAUSE - A suit, litigation or action before a court.

CAVEAT EMPTOR - Let the buyer beware. This term expresses the rule that the purchaser of an article must examine, judge, and test it for himself, being bound to discover any obvious defects or imperfections.

CERTIFICATE - A written representation that some legal formality has been complied with.

CERTIFIED COPY - Document certified by an official, such as a Notary, to be an accurate reproduction of an original.

CERTIORARI - To be informed of; the name of a writ issued by a superior court directing the lower court to send up to the former the record and proceedings of a case.

CHAIN OF KNOWLEDGE - Knowledge of identity linking the Notary with the signer through a credible identifying witness to establish the signer's identity. The Notary personally knows and can identify the credible witness, and the credible witness personally knows and can identify the document signer.

CHANGE OF VENUE - To remove place of trial from one place to another.

CHARGE - An obligation or duty; a formal complaint; an instruction of the court to the jury upon a case.

CHATTEL - An article of personal property.

CITATION - The act of the court by which a person is <u>summoned</u> or cited; also, reference to legal authority.

CIVIL(ACTIONS) - It indicates the private rights and remedies of individuals in contrast to the word "criminal" (actions) which relates to prosecution for violation of laws.

CLAIM (n.) - Any demand held or asserted as of right.

CODICIL - An addition to a will.

CODIFY - To arrange the laws of a country into a code.

COLLATERAL - By the side; accompanying; an article or thing given to secure performance of a promise.

COMITY - Courtesy; the practice by which one court follows the decision of another court on the same question.

COMMIT - To perform, as an act; to perpetrate, as a crime; to send a person to prison.

COMMON LAW - As distinguished from law created by the enactment of the legislature (called statutory law), it relates to those principles and rules of action which derive their authority solely from usages and customs of immemorial antiquity, particularly with reference to the ancient unwritten law of England. The written pronouncements of the common law are found in court decisions.

COMPLAINANT - One who applies to the court for legal redress.

COMPLAINT - The pleading of a plaintiff in a civil action; or a charge that a person has committed a specified offense.

COMPROMISE - An arrangement for settling a dispute by agreement.

CONDEMNATION - Taking private property for public use on payment therefor.

CONFESSION - Voluntary statement of guilt of crime.

CONFRONTATION - Witness testifying in presence of defendant.

CONSANGUINITY - Blood relationship.

CONSIGN - To give in charge; commit; entrust; to send or transmit goods to a merchant, factor, or agent for sale.

CONSIGNEE - One to whom a consignment is made.

CONSIGNOR - One who sends or makes a consignment.

CONSPIRACY - In criminal law, it means an agreement between two or more persons to commit an unlawful act.

CONSPIRATORS - Persons involved in a conspiracy.

CONSTITUENT – Any person who has the right to demand and receive services from an appointed or elected public official. This individual is not a client or a customer.

CONSTITUTION - The fundamental law of a nation or state.

CONSTRUE - To ascertain the meaning of language.

CONSUMMATE - To complete.

CONTINGENT - Possible, but not assured; dependent upon some condition.

CONTINUANCE - The adjournment or postponement of an action pending in a court.

CONTRACT - An agreement between two or more persons to do or not to do a particular thing.

CONTROVERT - To dispute, deny.

CONVERSION - Dealing with the personal property of another as if it were one's own, without right.

CONVEYANCE - An instrument transferring title to land.

CONVICTION - Generally, the result of a criminal trial which ends in a judgment-or sentence that the defendant is guilty as charged.

COPY CERTIFICATION – Notarial act in which a notary certifies that a copy of a document is a true and accurate reproduction of the original.

CORPUS DELICTI - The body of a crime; the crime itself.

CORROBORATE - To strengthen; to add weight by additional evidence.

COVENANT - Agreement.

CREDIBLE - Worthy of belief.

CREDIBLE WITNESS - A believable person who identifies a document signer to the notary public after taking an oath or affirmation. One credible witness must be known to the notary public and the credible witness must have satisfactory evidence of identification. Two credible witnesses must know the signer and the credible witnesses must have satisfactory evidence of identification. (Civil Code section 1185)

CREDITOR - A person to whom a debt is owing by another-person, called the "debtor."

CRIMINAL ACTION - Includes criminal proceedings.

CRITERIA (plural) - A means or tests for judging; a standard or standards.

CULPABLE - Blamable.

DAMAGES - A monetary compensation; - which may be recovered in the courts by any person who has suffered loss, or injury, whether to his person, property or rights through the unlawful act or omission or negligence of another.

DE FACTO - In fact; actually but without legal authority.

DE MINIMIS - Very small or trifling.

DE NOVO - Anew; afresh; a second time.

DEBT - A specified sum of money owing to one person from another, including not only the obligation of the debtor to pay, but the right of the creditor to receive and enforce payment.

DECEDENT - A dead person.

DECISION - A judgment or decree pronounced by a court in determination of a case.

DECLARANT - A person who makes a statement.

DECREE - An order of the court, determining the rights of all parties to a suit.

DEED - A writing containing a contract sealed and delivered; particularly to convey real property.

DEFAMATION - Injuring one's reputation by false statements.

DEFAULT - The failure to fulfill a duty, observe a promise, discharge an obligation, or perform an agreement.

DEFENDANT - The person defending or denying; the party against whom relief or recovery is sought in an action or suit.

DEFRAUD - To practice fraud; to cheat or trick.

DELEGATE (v.) - To entrust to the care or management of another.

DEMUR (v.) - To dispute the sufficiency in law of the pleading of the other side.

DENIAL - A form of pleading; refusing to admit the truth of a statement, charge, etc.

DEPONENT - One who gives oral testimony under oath that is later reduced to writing.

DEPOSITION - Testimony given under oath outside of court for use in court or for the purpose of obtaining information in preparation for trial of a case.

DETERIORATION - A degeneration such as from decay, corrosion or disintegration.

DETRIMENT - Any loss or harm to person or property.

DEVIATION - A turning aside.

DEVISE - A gift of real property by the last will and testament of the donor.

DICTA (plural) - Any statements made by the court in an opinion concerning some rule of law not necessarily involved nor essential to the determination of the case.

DICTUM (sing.) - An authoritative pronouncement

DIRECT EVIDENCE - Evidence that directly proves a fact, without an inference or presumption, and which in itself if true, conclusively establishes that fact.

DIRECT EXAMINATION - The first examination of a witness upon a matter that is not within the scope of a previous examination of the witness.

DISAFFIRM - To repudiate.

DISMISS - In an action or suit, it means to dispose of the case without any further consideration or hearing.

DISSENT - To denote disagreement of one or more judges of a court with the decision passed by the majority upon a case before them.

DOCTRINE - A rule, principle, theory of law.

DOCUMENT CUSTODIAN – Permanent keeper of an original document.

DOMICILE - That place where a man has his true, fixed and permanent home to which whenever he is absent he has the intention of returning.

DRAFT (n.) - A commercial paper ordering payment of money drawn by one

DRAWEE - The person who is requested to pay the money.

DRAWER - The person who draws the commercial paper and addresses it to the drawee.

DUPLICATE - A counterpart produced by the same impression as the original enlargements and miniatures, or by mechanical or electronic re-recording, or by chemical reproduction, or by other equivalent technique which accurately reproduces the original.

DURESS - Use of force to compel performance or non-performance of an act.

EASEMENT - A liberty, privilege, or advantage without profit, in the lands of another.

EGRESS - Act or right of going out or leaving; emergence.

EMBEZZLEMENT - To steal; to appropriate fraudulently to one's own use property entrusted to one's care.

EMINENT DOMAIN - The right of a state to take private property for public use.

ENACT - To make into a law.

ENDORSEMENT - Act of writing one's name on the back of a note, bill or similar written instrument.

ENJOIN - To require a person, by writ of injunction from a court of equity, to perform or to abstain or desist from some act.

ENTIRETY - The whole; that which the law considers as one whole, and not capable of being divided into parts.

ENTRAPMENT - Inducing one to commit a Crime so as to arrest him.

ENUMERATED - Mentioned specifically; designated.

EQUITY - In its broadest sense, this term denotes the spirit and the habit of fairness, justness, and right

ERROR - A mistake of law or the false or irregular application of law as will nullify the judicial proceedings.

ERRORS AND OMISSIONS INSURANCE - Contract between a Notary and an indemnity company whereby, in the event of a lawsuit against the Notary resulting from certain acts in performing a notarization, the company absorbs the Notary's costs and financial liabilities up to an agreed limit.

ESCROW - A deed, bond or other written engagement, delivered to a third person, to be delivered by him only upon the performance or fulfillment of some condition.

ESTATE - The interest which any one has in lands, or in any other subject of property.

ESTOP - To stop, bar, or impede.

ESTOPPEL - A rule of law which prevents a man from alleging or denying a fact, because of his own previous act.

ET AL. (alii) - And others.

ET SEQ. (sequential) - And the following.

ET UX. (uxor) - And wife.

EVIDENCE - Testimony, writings, material objects, or other things presented to the senses that are offered to prove the existence or nonexistence of a fact. Means from which inferences may be drawn as a basis of proof in duly constituted judicial or fact finding tribunals, and includes testimony in the form of opinion and hearsay.

EX POST FACTO, - After the fact.

EX PARTE - On one side only; by or for one.

EX POST FACTO LAW - A law passed after an act was done which retroactively makes such act a crime.

EX REL (relations) - Upon relation or information.

EXCEPTION - An objection upon a matter of law to a decision made, either before or after judgment by a court.

EXECUTOR (male) - A male who has been appointed by will to execute the will.

EXECUTORY - That which is yet to be executed or performed.

EXECUTRIX(female) - A female who has been appointed by will to execute the will.

EXEMPT - To release from some liability to which others are subject.

EXTRADITION - Surrender of a fugitive from one nation to another.

FABRICATE - To construct; to invent a false story.

FACSIMILE - An exact or accurate copy of an original instrument.

FEASANCE - The doing of an act.

FELONIOUS - Criminal, malicious.

FELONY - Generally, a criminal offense that may be punished by death or imprisonment for more than one year as differentiated from a misdemeanor.

FEME SOLE - A single woman.

FIDUCIARY - A person who is invested with rights and powers to be exercised for the benefit of another person.

FIERI FACIAS - A writ of execution commanding the sheriff to levy and collect the amount of a judgment from the goods and chattels of the judgment debtor.

FINDING OF FACT - Determination from proof or judicial notice of the existence of a fact. A ruling implies a supporting finding of fact; no separate or formal finding is required unless required by a statute of this state.

FISCAL - Relating to accounts or the management of revenue.

FORECLOSURE (sale) - A sale of mortgaged property to obtain satisfaction of the mortgage out of the sale proceeds.

FORFEITURE - A penalty, a fine.

FORGERY - Fabricating or producing falsely, counterfeited; such as false signature.

FORTUITOUS - Accidental.

FORUM - A court of justice; a place of jurisdiction.

FRAUD - Deception; trickery aimed at causing a person to unknowingly surrender money, property, rights or advantages without compensation.

FUNGIBLE - Of such kind or nature that one specimen or part may be used in the place of another.

GARNISHEE - Person garnished.

GARNISHMENT - A legal-process to reach the money or effects of a defendant, in the possession or control of a third person.

GRAND JURY - Not less than 16, not more than 23 citizens of a county sworn to inquire into crimes committed or triable in the county.

GRANT - To agree to; convey, especially real property.

GRANTEE - The person to whom a grant is made.

GRANTOR - The person by whom a grant is made.

GRATUITOUS - Given without a return, compensation or consideration.

GREEN CARD - Resident alien identification document (not actually green) issued by the U.S. Immigration and Naturalization Service, in the form of either the I-551 or the older I-151 card.

GUARANTY (n.) - A promise to answer for the payment of some debt, or the performance of some duty, in case of the failure of another person, who, in the first instance, is liable for such payment or performance.

GUARDIAN - The person, committee, or other representative authorized by law to protect the person or estate or both of an incompetent (or of a sui juris person having a guardian) and to act for him in matters affecting his person or property or both. An incompetent is a person under disability imposed by law.

GUILTY - Establishment of the fact that one has committed a breach of conduct; especially, a violation of law.

HABEAS CORPUS - You have the body, the name given to a variety of writs, having for their object to bring a party before a court or judge for decision as to whether such person is being lawfully held prisoner.

HEARSAY - A type of testimony given by a witness who relates, not what he knows personally, but what others have told him or what he has heard said by others.

HEARSAY RULE, THE - (a) "Hearsay evidence" is evidence of a statement that was made other than by a witness while testifying at the hearing and that is offered to prove the truth of the matter stated; (b) Ex-except as provided by law, hearsay evidence is inadmissible; (e) This section shall be known and may be cited as the hearsay rule.

HEIR - Generally, one who inherits property, real or personal.

HOLDER OF THE PRIVILEGE - (a) The client when he has no guardian or conservator; (b) A guardian or conservator of the client when the client has a guardian or conservator; (c) The personal representative of the client if the client is dead; (d) A successor, assign, trustee in dissolution, or any similar representative of a firm, association, organization, partnership, business trust, corporation, or public entity

HUSBAND-WIFE PRIVILEGE - An accused in a criminal proceeding has a privilege to prevent his spouse from testifying against him.

HYPOTHECATE - To pledge a thing without delivering it to the pledgee.

HYPOTHESIS - A supposition, assumption, or theory.

I

I.E. (id est.) - That is.

IB., OR IBID.(ibidem) - In the same place; used to refer to a legal reference previously cited to avoid repeating the entire citation.

ILLICIT - Prohibited; unlawful.

IMMUNITY - Exemption.

IMPEACH - To accuse, to dispute.

IMPLEAD - To sue or prosecute by due course of law.

IMPUTED - Attributed or charged to.

IN LOCO PARENTIS - In place of parent, a guardian.

INCOMMUNICADO - Denial of the right of a prisoner to communicate with friends or relatives.

INCOMPETENT - One who is incapable of caring for his own affairs because he is mentally deficient or undeveloped.

INCRIMINATION - A matter will incriminate a person if it constitutes, or forms an essential part of, or, taken in connection with other matters disclosed, is a basis for a reasonable inference of such a violation of the laws of this State as to subject him to liability to punishment therefor, unless he has become for any reason permanently immune from punishment for such violation.

INCUMBRANCE - Generally a claim, lien, charge or liability attached to and binding real property.

INDEMNIFY - To secure against loss or damage; also, to make reimbursement to one for a loss already incurred by him.

INDEMNITY - An agreement to reimburse another person in case of an anticipated loss falling upon him.

IDENTIFICATION – Knowing who a person is either by personal knowledge or proper identification.

INDICIA - Signs; indications.

INDICTMENT - An accusation in writing found and presented by a grand jury charging that a person has committed a crime.

INDORSE - To write a name on the back of a legal paper or document, generally, a negotiable instrument

INDUCEMENT - Cause or reason why a thing is done or that which incites the person to do the act or commit a crime; the motive for the criminal act.

INFANT - In civil cases one under 21 years of age.

INGRESS - The act of going into.

INJUNCTION - A writ or order by the court requiring a person, generally, to do or to refrain from doing an act.

INSOLVENT - The condition of a person who is unable to pay his debts.

INTERLOCUTORY - Temporary, not final; something intervening between the commencement and the end of a suit which decides some point or matter, but is not a final decision of the whole controversy.

INTERROGATORIES - A series of formal written questions used in the examination of a party or a witness usually prior to a trial.

INTESTATE - A person who dies without a will.

IPSO FACTO - By the fact itself; by the mere fact.

ISSUE (n.) - The disputed point or question in a case.

J

JEOPARDY - Danger, hazard, peril.

JOINDER - Joining; uniting with another person in some legal steps or proceeding.

JOURNAL NOTARIAL - Official record book, kept by notaries, showing all notarization performed.

JUDGMENT - The official decision of a court of justice.

JURAT - The clause written at the foot of an affidavit, stating when, where and before whom such affidavit was sworn.

JURISDICTION - The authority to hear and determine controversies between parties.

JURISPRUDENCE - The philosophy of law.

L

L.S. - Abbreviation of the Latin term locus sigilli, meaning "place of the seal." Traditional element indicating where the seal imprint is to be placed.

LACHES - The failure to diligently assert a right, which results in a refusal to allow relief.

LARCENY - Stealing personal property belonging to another.

LATENT - Hidden; that which does not appear on the face of a thing.

LAW - Includes constitutional, statutory, and decisional law.

LAWYER-CLIENT PRIVILEGE - (1) A "client" is a person, public officer, or corporation, association, or other organization or entity, either public or private, who is rendered professional legal services by a lawyer, or who consults a lawyer with a view to obtaining professional legal services from him; (2) A "lawyer" is a person authorized, or reasonably believed by the client to be authorized, to practice law in any state or nation; (3) A "representative of the lawyer" is one employed to assist the lawyer in the rendition of professional legal services; (4) A communication is "confidential" if not intended to be disclosed to third persons other than those to whom disclosure is in furtherance of the rendition of professional legal services to the client or those reasonably necessary for the transmission of the communication.

general rule of privilege- A client has a privilege to refuse to disclose and to prevent any other person from disclosing confidential communications made for the purpose of facilitating the rendition of professional legal services to the client, (1) between himself or his representative and his lawyer or his lawyer's representative, or (2) between his lawyer and the lawyer's representative, or (3) by him or his lawyer to a lawyer representing another in a matter of common interest, or (4) between representatives of the client or between the client and a representative of the client, or (5) between lawyers. representing the client.

LEASE - A contract by which one conveys real estate for a limited time usually for a specified rent; personal property also may be leased.

LEGITIMATE - Lawful.

LESSEE - One to whom a lease is given.

LESSOR - One who grants a lease

LEVY - A collecting or exacting by authority.

LIABLE - Responsible; bound or obligated in law or equity.

LIBEL (v.) - To defame or injure a person's reputation by a published

LIEN - A hold or claim which one person has upon the property of another as a security for some debt or charge.

LIQUIDATED - Fixed; settled.

LIS PENDENS - A pending civil or criminal action.

LITATION - A judicial controversy.

LITERAL - According to the language.

LITIGANT - A party to a lawsuit.

LIVING WILL: Written statement of a person's wishes concerning medical treatment in the event the signer has an illness or injury and is unable to give instructions on his or her own behalf.

LOCUS - A place.

LOCUS DELICTI - Place of the crime.

LOCUS POENITENTIAE - The abandoning or giving up of one's intention to commit some crime before it is fully completed or abandoning a conspiracy before its purpose is accomplished.

LOOSE CERTIFICATE - Notarial certificate wording on a separate sheet of paper that is attached to a document. Used when no wording is provided, when the provided certificate wording does not comply with state requirements, when there is no room for the seal on the document or when a preprinted certificate has already been used by another Notary.

MALFEASANCE - To do a wrongful act.

MALICE - The doing of a wrongful act intentionally without just cause or excuse.

MANDAMUS - The name of a writ issued by a court to enforce the performance of some public duty.

MANDATORY (adj.) - Containing a command.

MARSHALING - Arranging or disposing of in order.

MAXIM - An established principle or proposition.

MINISTERIAL - That which involves obedience to instruction, but demands no special discretion, judgment or skill.

MISAPPROPRIATE - Dealing fraudulently with property entrusted to one.

MISDEMEANOR - A crime less than a felony and punishable by a fine or imprisonment for less than one year.

MISFEASANCE - Improper performance of a lawful act.

MISREPRESENTATION - An untrue representation of facts.

MITIGATE - To make or become less severe, harsh.

MITTIMUS - A warrant of commitment to prison.

MOOT (adj.) - Unsettled, undecided, not necessary to be decided.

MORTGAGE - A conveyance of property upon condition, as security for the payment of a debt or the performance of a duty, and to become void upon payment or performance according to the stipulated terms.

MORTGAGEE - A person to whom property is mortgaged.

MORTGAGOR - One who gives a mortgage.

MOTION - In legal proceedings, a "motion" is an application, either written or oral, addressed to the court by a party to an action or a suit requesting the ruling of the court on a matter of law.

MUTUALITY - Reciprocation.

NEGLIGENCE - The failure to exercise that degrees of care which an ordinarily prudent person would exercise under like circumstances.

NEGOTIABLE (instrument) - Any instrument obligating the payment of money, which is transferable from one person to another by endorsement and delivery or by delivery only.

NEGOTIATE - To transact business; to transfer a negotiable instrument; to seek agreement for the amicable disposition of a controversy or case.

NOLLE PROSEQUI - A formal entry upon the record, by the plaintiff in a civil suit or the prosecuting officer in a criminal action, by which he declares that he "will no further prosecute" the case.

NOLO CONTENDERE - The name of a plea in a criminal action, having the same effect as a plea of guilty; but not constituting a direct admission of guilt.

NOMINAL - Not real or substantial.

NOMINAL DAMAGES - Award of a trifling sum where no substantial injury is proved to have been sustained.

NONFEASANCE - Neglect of duty.

NOVATION - The substitution of a new debt or obligation for an existing one.

OATH - Oath includes affirmation or declaration under penalty of perjury.

OATH OF OFFICE – Oath promising too faithfully discharge the duties of a particular office.

OBITER DICTUM - Opinion expressed by a court on a matter not essentially-involved in a case and hence not a decision; also called dicta. If plural, sum where no substantial injury.

OBJECT (v.) - To oppose as improper or illegal and referring the question of its propriety or legality to the court.

OBLIGATION - A legal duty, by which a person is bound to do or not to do a certain thing.

OBLIGEE - The person to whom an obligation is owed.

OBLIGOR - The person who is to perform the obligation.

OFFER (v.) - To present for acceptance or rejection. (n.)- A proposal to do a thing, usually a proposal to make a contract.

OFFICIAL INFORMATION - Information within the custody or control of a department or agency of the government the disclosure of which is shown to be contrary to the public interest.

OFFSET - A deduction.

ONUS PROBANDI - Burden of proof.

OPINION - The statement by a judge of the decision reached in a case, giving the law as applied to the case and giving reasons for the judgment; also a belief or view.

OPTION - The exercise of the power of choice; also a privilege existing in one person, for which he has paid money, which gives him the right to buy or sell real or personal property at a given price within a specified time.

ORDER - A rule or regulation; every direction of a court or judge made or entered in writing but not including a judgment.

ORDINANCE - Generally, a rule established by authority; also commonly used to designate the legislative acts of a municipal corporation.

ORIGINAL - Writing or recording itself or any counterpart intended to have the same effect by a person executing or issuing it. An "original" of a photograph includes the negative or any print therefrom. If data are stored in a computer or similar device, any printout or other output readable by sight, shown to reflect the data accurately, is an original. "

OVERT - Open, manifest.

PARENS PATRIAE - Sovereign power of a state to protect or be a guardian over children and incompetents.

PARITY - Equality in purchasing power between the farmer and other segments of the economy.

PAROL - Oral or Verbal.

PAROLE - To release one in prison before the expiration of his sentence, conditionally.

PARTITION - A legal division of real or personal property between one or more owners.

PARTNERSHIP - An association of two or more persons to carry on as co-owners a business for profit.

PATENT (adj. Evident.(n.) - A grant of some privilege, property, or authority, made by the government

PECULATION - Stealing.

PECUNIARY - Monetary.

PER SE - In itself; taken alone.

PEREMPTORY - Imperative; absolute.

PERJURY - To lie or state falsely under oath.

PERPETUITY - Perpetual existence; also the quality or condition of an estate limited so that it will not take effect or vest within the period fixed by law.

PERSONAL KNOWLEDGE -

PERSON - Includes a natural person, firm, association, organization, partnership, business trust, corporation, or public entity.

PERSONAL APPEARANCE – Appearing in person, face-to-face with the notary at the time of the notarization.

PERSONAL HONOR – Individual conscience.

PERSONAL KNOWLEDGE: Familiarity with an individual resulting from random interactions over a period of time sufficient to eliminate every reasonable doubt that the individual has the identity claimed.

PERSONAL PROPERTY - Includes money, goods, chattels, things in action, and evidences of debt. personal property also may be leased.

PETITION - An application in writing for an order of the court stating the circumstances upon which it is founded and requesting any order or other relief from a court.

PHOTOCOPY - Reproduction of a document made through exact photographic duplication of the original's image, rather than through approximation of its image by hand-copying or other methods.

PLAINTIFF - A person who brings a court action.

PLEA - A pleading in a suit or action.

PLEADINGS - Formal allegations made by the parties of their respective claims and defenses, for the judgment of the court.

PLEDGE - A deposit of personal property as a security for the performance of an act.

PLEDGEE - The party to whom goods are delivered in pledge.

PLEDGOR - The party delivering goods in pledge.

PLENARY - Full; complete.

POLICE POWER - Inherent power of the state or its political subdivisions to enact laws within constitutional limits to promote the general welfare of society or the community.

POSITIVE IDENTIFICATION – Proper valid identification or personal knowledge.

POST MORTEM - After death.

POWER OF ATTORNEY - A writing authorizing one to act for another.

PRELIMINARY FACT - Fact upon the existence or nonexistence of which depends the admissibility or inadmissibility of evidence. The phrase "the admissibility or inadmissibility of evidence" includes the qualification or disqualification of a person to be a witness and the existence or nonexistence of a privilege.

PREPONDERANCE - Outweighing.

PRESUMPTION - An assumption of fact resulting from a rule of law which requires such fact to be assumed from another fact or group of facts found or otherwise established in the action.

PRIMA FACIE CASE - A case where the evidence is very patent against the defendant..

PRIMA FACUE - At first sight.

PRINCIPAL - The source of authority or rights; a person primarily liable as differentiated from "principle" as a primary or basic doctrine.

PRO AND CON - For and against.

PRO RATA - Proportionally.

PROBATE - Relating to proof, especially to the proof of wills.

PROBATIVE - Tending to prove.

PROCEDURE - In law, this term generally denotes rules which are established by the Federal, State, or local Governments regarding the types of pleading and courtroom practice which must be followed by the parties involved in a criminal or civil case.

PROCLAMATION - A public notice by an official of some order, intended action, or state of facts.

PROFFERED EVIDENCE - The admissibility or inadmissibility of which is dependent upon the existence or nonexistence of a preliminary fact.

PROMISSORY (NOTE) - A promise in writing to pay a specified sum at an expressed time, or on demand, or at sight, to a named person, or to his order, or bearer.

PROOF - The establishment by evidence of a requisite degree of belief concerning a fact in the mind of the trier of fact or the court.

PROPERTY - Includes both real and personal property.

PROPRIETARY (adj.) - Relating or pertaining to ownership; usually a single owner.

PROSECUTE - To carry on an action or ' other judicial proceeding; to proceed against a person criminally.

PROVISO - A limitation or condition in a legal instrument.

PROXIMATE - Immediate; nearest

PUBLIC EMPLOYEE - An officer, agent, or employee of a public entity.

PUBLIC ENTITY - Includes a national, state, county, city and county, city, district, public authority, public agency, or any other political subdivision or public corporation, whether foreign or domestic.

PUBLIC OFFICIAL - Includes an official of a political subdivision of such state or territory and of a municipality.

PUNITIVE - Relating to punishment.

QUASH - To make void.

QUASI - As if; as it were.

QUID PRO QUO - Something for something; the giving of one valuable thing for another.

QUITCLAIM (v.) - To release or relinquish claim or title to, especially in deeds to realty.

QUO WARRANTO - A legal procedure to test an official's right to a public office or the right to hold a franchise, or to hold an office in a domestic corporation.

RATIFY - To approve and sanction.

RE JUDICATA - A thing judicially acted upon or decided.

REAL PROPERTY - Includes lands, tenements, and hereditaments.

REALTY - A brief term for real property.

REBUT - To contradict; to refute, especially by evidence and arguments.

RECEIVER - A person who is appointed by the court to receive, and hold in trust property in litigation.

RECIDIVIST - Habitual criminal.

RECIPROCAL - Mutual.

RECOUPMENT - To keep back or get something which is due; also, it is the right of a defendant to have a deduction from the amount of the plaintiff's damages because the plaintiff has not fulfilled his part of the same contract.

RECROSS EXAMINATION - Examination of a witness by a cross-examiner subsequent to a redirect examination of the witness.

REDEEM - To release an estate or article from mortgage or pledge by paying the debt for which it stood as security.

REFEREE - A person to whom a cause pending in a court is referred by the court, to take testimony, hear the parties, and report thereon to the court.

REFERENDUM - A method of submitting an important legislative or administrative matter to a direct vote of the people.

RELEVANT EVIDENCE - Evidence including evidence relevant to the credulity of a witness or hearsay declarant, having any tendency in reason to prove or disprove any disputed fact that is of consequence to the determination of the action.

REMAND - To send a case back to the lower court from which it came, for further proceedings.

REPLEVIN - An action to recover goods or chattels wrongfully taken or detained.

REPLY (REPLICATION) - Generally, a reply is what the plaintiff or other person who has instituted proceedings says in answer to the defendant's case.

RES ADJUDICATA - Doctrine that an issue or dispute litigated and determined in a case between the opposing parties is deemed permanently decided between these parties.

RESCIND (RESCISSION) - To avoid or cancel a contract.

RESPONDENT - A defendant in a proceeding in chancery or admiralty; also, the person who contends against the appeal in a case.

RESTITUTION - In equity, it is the restoration of both parties to their original condition (when practicable), upon the rescission of a contract for fraud or similar cause.

RETROACTIVE (RETROSPECTIVE) - Looking back; effective as of a prior time.

REVERSED - A term used by appellate courts to indicate that the decision of the lower court in the case before it has been set aside.

REVOKE - To recall or cancel.

RIPARIAN (RIGHTS) - The rights of a person owning land containing or bordering on a water course or other body of water, such as lakes and rivers.

S.S. - Abbreviations of the Latin word scilicet, meaning "in particular" or "namely." Traditional element appearing after or to the right of the venue in a notarial certificate.

SALE - A contract whereby the owner

SANCTION - A penalty or punishment provided as a means of enforcing obedience to a law; also, an authorization.

SATISFACTION - The discharge of an obligation by paying a party what is due to him; or what is-awarded to him by the judgment of a court or otherwise.

SCINTILLA - A spark; also the least particle.

SECURITY - Indemnification; the term is applied to an obligation, such as a mortgage or deed of trust, given by a debtor to insure the payment or performance of his debt, by furnishing the creditor with a resource to be used in case of the debtor's failure to fulfill the principal obligation.

SENTENCE - The judgment formally pronounced by the court or judge upon the defendant after his conviction in a criminal prosecution.

SIGNATURE BY MARK - An "X" or other symbol made in place of a signature by a person unable to write and witnessed by a Notary and two other people.

SITUS - Location.

SOVEREIGN - A person, body or state in which independent and supreme authority is vested.

STARE DECISIS - To follow decided cases.

STATE - "State" means this State, unless applied to the different parts of the United States. In the latter case, it includes any state, district, commonwealth, territory or insular possession of the United States, including the District of Columbia.

STATEMENT - (a) Oral or written verbal expression or (b) nonverbal conduct of a person intended by him as a substitute for oral or written verbal expression.

STATUTE - An act of the legislature includes a treaty.

STATUTE OF LIMITATION - A statute limiting the time to bring an action after the right of action has arisen.

STAY - To hold in abeyance an order of a court.

STIPULATION - Any agreement made by opposing attorneys regulating any matter incidental to the proceedings or trial.

SUBSCRIBED - Signed

SUBORDINATION (AGREEMENT) - An agreement making one's rights inferior to or of a lower rank than another's.

SUBORNATION - The crime of procuring a person to lie or to make false statements to a court.

SUBPOENA - A writ or order directed to a person, and requiring his attendance at a particular time and place to testify as a witness.

SUBPOENA DUCES TECUM - A subpoena used, not only for the purpose of compelling witnesses to attend in court, but also requiring them to bring with them books or documents which may be in their possession, and which may tend to elucidate the subject matter of the trial.

SUBROGATION - The substituting of one for another as a creditor, the new creditor succeeding to the formers rights.

SUBSCRIBING WITNESS EXECUTION – Notarial act where a subscribing witness states under oath or affirmation that he or she witnessed the principal sign a document and that they signed it as a witness.

SUBSIDY - A government grant to assist a private enterprise deemed advantageous to the public.

SUI GENERIS - Of the same kind.

SUIT - Any civil proceeding by a person or persons against another or others in a court of justice by which the plaintiff pursues the remedies afforded him by law.

SUMMONS - A notice to a defendant that an action against him has been commenced and requiring him to appear in court and answer the complaint.

SUPRA - Above; this word occurring by itself in a book refers the reader to a previous part of the book.

SUPREME BEING – God or other entity or object of faith and worship.

SURETY - A person who binds himself for the payment of a sum of money, or for the performance of something else, for another.

SURPLUSAGE - Extraneous or unnecessary matter.

SURVIVORSHIP - A term used when a person becomes entitled to property by reason of his having survived another person who had an interest in the property.

SUSPEND SENTENCE - Hold back a sentence pending good behavior of prisoner.

SWEAR – To make an oath or affirmation; to state under oath or affirmation.

SYLLABUS - A note prefixed to a report, especially a case, giving a brief statement of the court's ruling on different issues of the case.

T

TENANT - One who holds or possesses lands by any kind of right or title; also, one who has the temporary use and occupation of real property owned by another person (landlord),the duration and terms of his tenancy being usually fixed by an instrument called "a lease."

TENDER - An offer of money; an expression of willingness to perform a contract according to its terms.

TERM - When used with reference to a court, it signifies the period of time during which the court holds a session, usually of several weeks or months duration.

TESTAMENTARY - Pertaining to a will or the administration of a will.

TESTATOR (male) - One who makes or has made a testament or will.

TESTATRIX(female) - One who makes or has made a testament or will.

TESTIFY (TESTIMONY) - To give evidence under oath as a witness.

TORT - Wrong; injury to the person.

TRESPASS - Entry into another's ground, illegally.

TRIAL - The examination of a cause, civil or criminal, before a judge who has jurisdiction over it, according to the laws of the land.

TRIER OF FACT - Includes (a) the jury and (b) the court when the court is trying an issue of fact other than one relating to the admissibility of evidence.

TRUST - A right of property, real or personal, held by one party for the benefit of another.

TRUSTEE - One who lawfully holds property in custody for the benefit of another.

ULTRA VIRES - Acts beyond the scope and power of a corporation, association, etc.

UNAVAILABLE AS A WITNESS - The declarant is (1) Exempted or precluded on the ground of privilege from testifying concerning the matter to which his statement is relevant; (2) Disqualified from testifying to the matter; (3) Dead or unable to attend or to testify at the hearing because of then existing physical or mental illness or infirmity; (4) Absent from the hearing and the court is unable to compel his attendance by its process; or (5) Absent from the hearing and the proponent of his statement has exercised reasonable diligence but has been unable to procure his attendance by the court's process.

UNILATERAL - One-sided; obligation upon, or act of one party.

USURY - Unlawful interest on a loan.

VACATE - To set aside; to move out.

VARIANCE - A discrepancy or disagreement between two instruments or

VENDEE - A purchaser or buyer.

VENDOR - The person who transfers property by sale, particularly real estate; the term "seller" is used more commonly for one who sells personal property.

VENUE - The place at-which an action is tried, generally based on locality or judicial district in which an injury occurred or a material fact happened.

VERDICT - The formal decision or finding of a jury.

VERIFICATION – A declaration that a statement or pleading is true.

VERIFY - To confirm or substantiate by oath.

VEST - To accrue to.

VOID - Having no legal force or binding effect.

VOIR DIRE - Preliminary examination of a witness or a juror to test competence, interest, prejudice, etc.

WAIVE - To give up a right.

WAIVER - The intentional or voluntary relinquishment of a known right.

WARRANT (n.) - A writ issued by a judge, or other competent authority, addressed to a sheriff, or other officer, requiring him to arrest the person therein named, and bring him before the judge or court to answer or be examined regarding the offense with which he is charged.

WARRANT (WARRANTY) (v.) - To promise that a certain fact or state of facts, in relation to the subject matter, is, or shall be, as it is represented to.

WILL: Legal document containing a person's wishes about disposition of personal property after death; short for "last will and testament."

WILLINGNESS – Acting voluntarily without duress or undue influences.

WITNESS – One who has personally observed something.

WRIT - An order or process issued in the name of the sovereign or in the name of a court or judicial officer, commanding the performance or nonperformance of some act.

WRITING - Handwriting, typewriting, printing, photostatting, photographing and every other means of recording upon any tangible thing any form of communication or representation, including letters, words, pictures, sounds, or symbols, or combinations thereof.

writing. (n.)- The initial pleading on the part of the plaintiff in an admiralty proceeding.

WRITINGS AND RECORDINGS - Consists of letters, words, or numbers, or their equivalent, set down by handwriting, typewriting, printing, photostatting, photographing, magnetic impulse, mechanical or electronic recording, or other form of data compilation.

YELLOW DOG CONTRACT - A contract by which employer requires employee to sign an instrument promising as condition that he will not join a union during its continuance, and will be discharged if he does join.

ZONING - The division of a city by legislative regulation into districts and the prescription and application in each district of regulations having to do with structural and architectural designs of buildings and of regulations prescribing use to which buildings within designated districts may be put.

NOTARY PUBLIC FREQUENTLY ASKED QUESTIONS

1. How do I become a Notary Public?

You must first be at least 18 years of age and a legal resident of the State of California. Satisfactorily complete a course of study approved by the Secretary of State. Take and pass an examination about notary law, pass your background investigation, file your bond with the county clerk and take your oath of office. (Government Code section 8201)

2. I did not file my oath and bond on time, what do I do?

• If you failed to file your oath and bond within the prescribed time, your commission is void.

• If you are a new applicant and took an approved six-hour notary public education course, you must attach a current proof of completion certificate to a new application, along with a 2" x 2" color passport photo of yourself and a check for twenty dollars ($20). You will also need to have your fingerprints retaken at a Live Scan site.

• If you are a notary public seeking reappointment and took an approved three-hour notary public refresher education course, you will still need to take an approved six-hour course. The three-hour course no longer meets the education requirements because your current commission has expired. You will need to attach the proof of completion certificate for the six-hour course to a new application, along with a 2" x 2" color passport photo of yourself and a check for twenty dollars ($20). You will also need to have your fingerprints retaken at a Live Scan site.

3. Can I notarize for a stranger with no identification?

Yes, if a credible witness accompanies the stranger.

4. If two people sign the same document, do I charge one or two fees?

The fee is per signature/person even if the notary public is using one notarial certificate, the notary public in this case is identifying and witnessing two separate executions on the document.

5.   May I correct a mistake I made in a notary certificate several days after it was executed?

No, any corrections must be made at the original time of notarization before the constituent leaves.

6.   Am I required to be bonded or have liability (errors and omissions) insurance?

California law requires it's notaries public to be bonded but liability insurance is optional. Having errors and omissions insurance is left to the discretion of the notary public. Liability insurance protects the notary public from the public. Bonding protects the constituent (customer) from the notary public.

7.   If I change my business or home address, what should I do?

Notify the secretary of state within 30 days using certified mail (return receipt requested).

8.   Can I certify a copy of a birth or death certificate?

No, as a notary there are only 2 items that you are authorized to certify – one is your own records and the other is a power of attorney.

9.   If I lose my stamp or journal, what should I do?

Notify the Secretary of State immediately by certified mail (return receipt requested) and explain the circumstances surrounding what happened. If applicable, include a photocopy of a police report. Upon request the Secretary of State will send you a new authorization to manufacture a notary public seal. (Government Code section 8207.3)

10.   I received a phone call requesting a photocopy of an entry in my journal. Do I have to comply?

No, all request must be in writing and must give the individual's name, the type of transaction and the month and year of the transaction. With this information you can release the line item that was requested at a fee not greater than .30 per page.

EXAMINATION SECTION – TEST 1

DIRECTIONS: Each question or incomplete statement is followed by four possible answers. Select the BEST possible answer or word that completes the question or statement. *CIRCLE THE MOST CORRECT ANSWER.*

1. **A notary public who advertises as an immigration specialist may advertise that he or she is a notary in:**

    A. Newspaper ads only

    B. Newspaper and other ads

    C. May not advertise as a notary

    D. Only when a notice is posted

2. **A California notary is authorized to certify copies of:**

    A. Deeds

    B. Birth certificates

    C. Immigration documents

    D. None of the above

3. **The kind of document that assures that the constituent signed before *(in the presence of)* a notary public is guaranteed in:**

    A. Avenue

    B. Jurat

    C. An affidavit

    D. A contract

4. **A person who makes a sworn statement before a notary is:**

    A. An affiant

    B. A respondent

    C. A plaintiff

    D. A acknowledger

5. **California notaries may notarize anywhere within:**

    A. The county where they physically are

    B. The United States

    C. The state of California

    D. The county where they work

6. **A California notary may:**

    A. Notarize depositions and affidavits

    B. Administer oaths and affirmations

    C. Certify copies of powers of attorney

    D All of the above

7. **In an acknowledgment the notary does not certify:**

    A. The official capacity of the individual

    B. That the signer appeared before the notary

    C. That the signer acknowledged signing the document

    D. That the signer was positively identified

8. **Satisfactory evidence of identity can be best established by checking:**

    A. A social security card

    B. A current driver's license

    C. A resident alien card

    D. Personal Knowledge

9. **A notary may pre-sign acknowledgments only in the following case:**

    A. If the notary is going out of town

    B. If another notary is going to complete the form

    C. A notary may never pre-sign acknowledgments

    D. If it is an emergency

10. **The most frequent notarial act is the:**

    A. Acknowledgment

    B. Jurat

    C. Copy certification

    D. Protest

11. **The maximum fee for an acknowledgment is:**

    A. $15 per signature

    B. $5 per signature

    C. $10 per document

    D. A fee that is reasonable and agreed upon

12. **A person appearing before a notary is called:**

      A. An affiant

      B. A constituent

      C. An affirmant

      D. A client

13. **The words "subscribed and sworn to" indicate which kind of notarial certificate is being completed:**

      A. A jurat certificate

      B. An all-purpose acknowledgment certificate

      C. A certification for a copy certification

      D. A subscribing witness certificate

14. **Documents that in the notary's <u>opinion</u> are incomplete (based on knowledge and prior experience) may be notarized in the following case:**

      A. If the notary knows the constituent personally

      B. Incomplete documents must not be notarized

      C. If the notary's employer instructs the notary to do it

      D. If the constituent assures the notary, under oath, that the document is complete

15. **The notary journal must include all of the following information except:**

      A. A copy of the document notarized

      B. The identification that was used

      C. The fee charged by the notary

      D. The signature of the person requesting the notary service

16. **For an identification card to be valid it must contain all but the following:**

      A. Photograph

      B. Physical description

      C. Signature

      D. Thumb print

17. **To establish proper identification, the notary must have:**

   A. One primary ID

   B. One primary ID or two supplemental ID's

   C. One primary ID and one supplemental ID

   D. Two supplemental ID's

18. **If presented with a document which purports to be a will, the notary:**

   A. Must notarize the document

   B. Should decline and advise the person requesting the notarization to consult a member of the California State Bar

   C. Refer the constituent to another notary who is more knowledgeable

   D. Notarize the document taking special care

19. **The negligence of a notary may result in:**

   A. A civil action against the notary

   B. A misdemeanor or felony charge

   C. Fines from the state of California

   D. Any of the above

20. **The main purpose of an acknowledgment is:**

   A. To provide positive identification

   B. To compel truthfulness

   C. To deter fraud

   D. None of the above

21. **The word(s) the law uses to describe the form of a notary journal is:**

   A. Permanently bound

   B. Loose leaf

   C. Sequential

   D. Hard bound

22. **You may notarize documents from other states:**

   A. As long as you and the constituents are in California

   B. As long as you are in the other state

   C. As long as you are a resident of the other state

   D. As long as you personally know the constituent

23. **The most important determinant in deciding to notarize for a signer who presents a document written in a foreign language is:**

   A. The signer's ability to communicate with the notary

   B. The signer's ability to write his signature in english

   C. The signer appearing before the notary

   D. The signer's ability to present proper ID

24. **A notary must use the official seal in all cases, except:**

   A. There are no exceptions to this rule

   B. When performing acknowledgments for California subdivision map certificates

   C. When a seal and a rubber stamp is used at the same time

   D. When you type the information instead

25. **Which of the following is not true about the notary's seal?:**

   A. It must contain the name of the notary

   B. It must contain the California State Seal

   C. It must contain the commission expiration date

   D. It must contain the notary's social security number

26. **Which of the following would a notary not consider an acceptable form of identification?:**

   A. Government issued ID such as a driver's license or passport.

   B. Credible witness

   C. Birth certificate

   D. Two credible witnesses

27. **Which one of the following IDs would be acceptable to a California notary?:**

   A. Employee ID that was issued by your private employer

   B. School ID that was issue by your school

   C. Social Security card issued by the Department of Social Security

   D. Inmate ID card as long as the inmate is in custody

28. **When a notary changes employment s/he must surrender their seal and journal to:**

> A. The county clerk
>
> B. The Secretary of State
>
> C. To the employer
>
> D. None of the above

29. **If you are notarizing a document for a relative or a close friend which of the following items must be included in your journal?:**

> A. The notary fee paid
>
> B. A copy of the signers birth certificate
>
> C. Your relationship to the individual
>
> D. The length of time that you have known the individual

30. **Which one of the following documents can be notarized without the use of your official seal?:**

> A. A subdivision map
>
> B. A Deed of Trust
>
> C. A Quitclaim Deed
>
> D. A Deed of Reconveyance

EXAMINATION SECTION – TEST 2

DIRECTIONS: Each question or incomplete statement is followed by four possible answers. Select the BEST possible answer or word that completes the question or statement. *CIRCLE THE MOST CORRECT ANSWER.*

1.   **The *primary* duty of a Notary Public is to:**

      A. Administer oaths, and take proof and acknowledgment of written instruments

      B. Attest to the genuineness of any deeds or writings in order to render them available as evidence of the facts therein contained

      C. Take acknowledge of or proof of the execution of an instrument by his client in respect to any matter, claim or proceeding

      D. Attest to the genuineness of notice, in that one who is entitled to notice of a fact will thus be bound by acquiring knowledge of it.

2.   **How is the __maximum__ fee to which a notary is entitled set?:**

      A. Each notary sets his own fee

      B. The fee is determined by agreement

      C. By law

      D. There is no fee

3.   **Who appoints and commissions notaries public?:**

      A. Attorney General

      B. Commissioner of General Services

      C. Secretary of State

      D. Governor

4.   **The JURAT is:**

      A. Evidence of the truth of the matters in relation to which he certifies

      B. Evidence that the oath was properly taken before a duly authorized officer

      C. A part of the oath

      D. Conclusive evidence of an oath's due administration

5. **A notary public who practices any <u>fraud</u> or deceit in the performance of his or her duties can be convicted of:**

   A. Misconduct

   B. A misdemeanor or a felony, depends on the specific act

   C. Fraud

   D. Treason

6. **The law requires all commissioned notaries to file a bond in the amount of $15,000 with the county clerks office within _____ days of the commission date:**

   A. 30 days

   B. 45 days

   C. 60 days

   D. No time limit

7. **Can a notary public notarize a sworn statement if the person refuses to take the oath "swear to God" because of religious reasons?**

   A. No, not under any circumstances

   B. Yes, it can still be notarized without the sworn statement

   C. No, unless the person provides a statement explaining why their religion prevents them from taking an oath.

   D. Yes, as long as the person "affirms" that the facts stated are true to the best of his/her knowledge

8. **The place on a notary certificate that gives the location where the notarial act was performed is called the:**

   A. Scilicet

   B. Venue

   C. Testimonium clause

   D. Verification

9. **A notary public may lawfully:**

   A. Execute an acknowledgment to a will

   B. Take an acknowledge to a legal instrument in which he has a financial interest

   C. Take the acknowledgment of his constituent

   D. Take the acknowledgment of a third party

10.   **A notary public is NOT permitted to administer an oath to:**

     A. A military officer

     B. A public official

     C. A member of his family

     D. Himself

11.   **When an appointee does not file his oath of office within the specified time period:**

     A. His commission does not take effect

     B. His fee is refunded

     C. He is required to pass another examination for the same appointment

     D.He is guilty of a misdemeanor

12.   **All persons commissioned as notaries public:**

     A. Must be native born citizens

     B. Must have high school diplomas

     C. Are commissioned at the discretion of the Secretary of State

     D. Must have some legal background

13.   **If there is no room on a document for a notary seal:**

     A. The seal may be affixed to a certificate and attached to the document

     B. The seal may be affixed over the notary's signature

     C. The seal may be affixed on the back of the document

     D. The seal may be omitted

14.   **A notary public CANNOT give legal advice EXCEPT when he:**

     A. Makes known the fact that he is not an attorney

     B. Does not collect a fee

     C. Is also an attorney

     D. Finds it necessary to properly perform his duties as notary

15.   **A JURAT is added to:**

     A. A certificate

     B. An affidavit

     C. A certificate of authority

     D. An attestation

16. **A person who receives services from a notary public is properly termed a:**

    A. Client

    B. Advocate

    C. Constituent

    D. Buyer

17. **The Secretary of State may refuse to appoint any person as notary public or may revoke or suspend the commission of any notary public convicted of a felony or a lessor offense involving moral turpitude:**

    A. In any state or territory of the United States

    B. In the county of Jurisdiction

    C. In any county within the state

    D. In the state, if the conviction occurred after the age of 21

18. **Which of the following may be an impediment to a person being appointed to the office of notary public?:**

    A. Illegally using or carrying a pistol

    B. Receiving or having criminal possession of stolen property

    C. Unlawful possession of a habit forming narcotic drug

    D. All of the above

19. **An affiant who swears falsely may be prosecuted for:**

    A. Fraud

    B. Perjury

    C. Forgery

    D. Misrepresentation

20. **The Notary Public Institute recommends that the signature of the notary public should be made with:**

    A. Blue ink

    B. Black ink

    C. Blue or black ink

    D. Any color ink

21.   **A notarization must contain which of the below:**

      A. Address of the notary

      B. Secretary of state's facsimile signature

      C. Jurisdiction

      D. Commission expiration date

22.   **If a loose leaf certificate is to be attached to a document, it should be stapled:**

      A. In the upper left-hand corner of the front page only

      B. Over the blank space beneath the signatures

      C. To the margins only

      D. Anywhere on the document

23.   **The notary's certification that a party appeared before him/her, took an oath, and signed an affidavit is the:**

      A. Jurat

      B. Attestation

      C. Statement

      D. Acknowledgment

24.   **If there is neither a blank space or a margin, on a document, that is large enough for the placement of your entire stamp impression, the notary should then attempt to place a seal:**

      A. Over information that is handwritten

      B. Over information that is printed

      C. Over information that is typewritten

      D. On a separate, attached loose leaf certificate

25.   **If a notary is required to be bonded, the _____ is/are specified as surety or sureties:**

      A. Parties to any agreements notarized by the bonded notary

      B. Bonding company

      C. County

      D. Secretary of State

26. **The principal (document signer) does not have to sign in the presence of the notary if the service being provided is for a:**

   A. Acknowledgment

   B. Jurat

   C. A Living Trust

   D. A Security Agreement

27. **The term Venue refers to:**

   A. The state and city where the notary filed his/her bond

   B. The state and city where the document was prepared

   C. The state and county where the notary filed his/her bond

   D. The state and county where the notarization took place

28. **A notary should not notarize the following document unless s/he is advised to do so by an attorney:**

   A. A will

   B. A Living Trust

   C. A Power of Attorney

   D. A Warranty Deed

29. **California notaries must be at least _____ years old to be appointed:**

   A. 18

   B. 19

   C. 20

   D. There is no minimum age limit

30. **The term of office for a California State Notary is:**

   A. 2 years

   B. 4 years

   C. 6 years

   D. 8 years

EXAMINATION SECTION TEST 3

DIRECTIONS: Each question or incomplete statement is followed by four possible answers. Select the BEST possible answer or word that completes the question or statement. *CIRCLE THE MOST CORRECT ANSWER.*

1. **A notary should NEVER, under any circumstances, notarize:**

   A. The signature of a business associate

   B. His/her own signature

   C. A unilateral contract

   D. The signature of a close relative

2. **A notary public who acts before taking and filing his or her oath of office and filing his bond is guilty of:**

   A. Malpractice

   B. Perjury

   C. A misdemeanor or a felony, depending on the type of document the notary public notarized.

   D. Fraud

3. *Witness my* **hand and** *seal* **is a short form of the:**

   A. Jurat

   B. Oath

   C. Notarization

   D. Testimonium clause

4. **State courts regard a notary's violation of duty as:**

   A. Serious professional misconduct

   B. Intentional misrepresentation

   C. Malpractice

   D. Malfeasance

5. **Satisfactory evidence of identity means reliance on:**

   A. A valid government issued ID card

   B. Government issued ID cards or personal knowledge

   C. A credible witness or personal knowledge

   D. All of the above are acceptable

6. **A lost or damaged seal:**

    A. Must be reported to the Secretary of State immediately by certified mail

    B. Must be reported to the Secretary of State within 30 days

    C. It is not mandatory that you notify the Secretary of State

    D. Must be replaced and them you must notify the Secretary of State

7. **Signature by Mark (X) is an acceptable signature if a person cannot write their name:**

    A. If there are two witnesses and one of them writes the signers name next to his mark.

    B. This is never an acceptable signature for accepting this document

    C. The service can only be completed if the document being notarized is a deed of trust

    D. This service can only be completed if the document being notarized is not a deed of trust.

8. **The county in which an affidavit is sworn is known as a(n):**

    A. Venue

    B. Juris

    C. Arena

    D. Quadrangle

9. **Which of the following statements is TRUE?:**

    A. During such time as a notary public is available as a notary, he/she may not engage in other business during that same time.

    B. A notary may be imprisoned for misuse of notarial powers.

    C. The notary does not have to consider whether the affidavit is correct or false if the affiant is duly administered and takes an oath.

    D. An affirmation is less legally binding than an oath sworn on a Bible.

10. **Once an individual's commission has been approved, the notary is required to:**

    A. Obtain errors and omissions insurance in the amount of $15,000 in order to protect the public.

    B. File an oath within 30 days with the county clerk in the county in which

    C. Obtain an official seal from a manufacturer approved by the Secretary of State.

    D. None of the above.

11. **Commissioned notaries in California who have completed the process of filing an oath and bond with the county clerk are permitted to notarize documents:**

    A. For anyone as long as both parties are in California.

    B. For any court ordered documents.

    C. For anyone within the county where the notary has his or her oath and bond on file as long as the signer can present proper identification and pay for the services.

    D. For anyone within the State of California as long as the document originated in California.

12. **Each of the following is an element of a typical certificate of acknowledgment EXCEPT:**

    A. County where notarization occurred

    B. Personal appearance of the signer

    C. Notary bond number

    D. Venue

13. **The public official whose duties include keeping records of all notaries in the state is the:**

    A. Secretary of state

    B. Pronotary

    C. Secretary of the <u>interior</u>

    D. County clerk

14. **The notary is required to obtain a thumbprint in his journal if the document being notarized is a:**

    A. Security agreement

    B. Any deed affecting real property or powers of attorney

    C. Living Will

    D. Immigration document

15. **The notary seal must contain which of the following elements:**

    A. The California state seal

    B. The Notaries public commission expiration date

    C. The county where the notary public is registered

    D. All of the above

16. **Of the following, which one would be more likely to take an oath rather than an affirmation? A(n):**

    A. Member of a religious order

    B. Attorney admitted to the bar

    C. Person swearing to a legal instrument

    D. Notary public

17. **A rubber stamp should NEVER be used:**

    A. To add information to that provided by the seal embosser

    B. To disclose the notary's office or residence address

    C. For recording the notary's name

    D. For creating a facsimile of the notary's signature

18. **The purpose of an affirmation is to:**

    A. Establish that the notary is personally acquainted with a part

    B. Certify the authenticity of a written document

    C. Uphold a notary's legal authority

    D. Serve as the legal equivalent to an oath

19. **An attorney submitted a written request to a notary public for a copy of his journal entry. What information must the notary receive prior to granting her request?**

    A. The month, day and year of the notarization, the name of the party document and the type of document to be notarized.

    B. The month and year of the notarization, the name of the party, the type of document notarized

    C. The year of notarization, the name of the party, the type of document and the type of identifying document used for verification

    D. The month and year of the notarization, the name of the party and the type of identifying document used for verification

20.   **The California notary public seal must be:**

        A. Photographically reproducible

        B. Obtained and used by notaries public

        C. Always used with an embosser

        D. Both a & b

21.   **A notary's general authority is defined in the:**

        A. Government Code

        B. Public Officers Law

        C. Executive Law

        D. Civil Practice Law and Rules

22.   **A notary is not entitled to a fee for administering the oath of office to a(n):**

        A. Military officer

        B. Clerk of the poll

        C. Public official

        D. None of the above

23.   **The fee for re-taking a failed examination is:**

        A. Nothing

        B. $1.00

        C. $40.00

        D. $20.00

24.   **Which of the following statements concerning the taking of oaths is NOT true? The:**

        A. Person must swear in the notary's presence

        B. Notary must conscientiously take upon himself the obligation of the oath

        C. Person must swear that what he states is true

        D. Person does not necessarily have to swear before God

25.   **A notary may NOT take the acknowledgment or proof of any party to a written instrument executed by a corporation in which he is a:**

        A. Major stockholder

        B. Director

        C. Officer

        D. All of the above

26.   **If you change your address you must notify the Secretary of State by certified mail within:**

   A. 15 days

   B. 30 days

   C. 45 days

   D. There is no time limit

27.   **A notary that has a direct or beneficial interest in a transaction may not notarize any documents related to that transaction unless s/he:**

   A. Has written approval from all parties connected to the transaction

   B. S/he has been a practicing notary for at least 8 years

   C. Has a valid bond of at least $15,000 in place

   D. There are no exceptions

28.   **If a notary willingly and knowingly notarizes a real estate document that they know to be fraudulent, they are guilty of a:**

   A. Misdemeanor

   B. Lis Pendes

   C. Carpe diem

   D. Felony

29.   **If you present yourself as a notary without holding a valid commission you are guilty of a:**

   A. A felony

   B. A misdemeanor

   C. A $50.00 fine

   D. There is no law against impersonating a notary

30.   **A notary that knowingly completes a fraudulent deed of trust, on a one to four unit house, is guilty of:**

   A. A misdemeanor

   B. A felony

   C. A violation of state statue

   D. A violation of federal statue

EXAMINATION SECTION - TEST 4

DIRECTIONS: Each question or incomplete statement is followed by four possible answers. Select the BEST possible answer or word that completes the question or statement. *CIRCLE THE MOST CORRECT ANSWER.*

1.   **Fees for any one set of immigration documents are restricted to:**

    A. $15

    B. $8

    C. $5

    D. $3

2.   **When do you officially become a notary public?**

    A. When you pass the state exam.

    B. When the Secretary of State sends you your commission.

    C. When you complete your first notarization.

    D. After you receive your commission, take your oath, and file your bond.

3.   **In their jurisdictions, notaries must serve:**

    A. County resident only

    B. State resident only

    C. U.S. citizens only

    D. All persons that have a legal and proper request and can pay their fees

4.   **The notary's signature:**

    A. Should be written in his own hand

    B. Can be written by a designated person

    C. Should be stamped on each notarial certificate

    D. Should itself be notarized

5.   **The act of notarization:**

    A. Guarantees the truth of statements in a document

    B. Assures that a document's signers signature is authentic

    C. Guarantees the legality of a document

    D. Provides positive proof that a signer is honest

6.   The main purpose of acknowledgment before a Notary is to:

>   A. Prove satisfactory evidence of a document signer

>   B. Appeal to the conscience of a document signer

>   C. Subject a document signer to criminal penalties for falsehood

>   D. Point out and record flaws in a legal document

7.   The letters "ss" that appear in the venue portion of a notarial certificate stand for:

>   A. Social Security Number

>   B. The Latin word scilicet

>   C. Single sources

>   D. Save Our Ship

8.   The California residency requirement to apply to become a notary is:

>   A. One year

>   B. Thirty days

>   C. Twenty-four hours

>   D. There is NO residency time requirement in California

9.   A phone call can establish personal appearance:

>   A. Only when the Notary is personally familiar with the signature

>   B. If a business relationship with the signer has been established

>   C. At the time of notarization, but not before and not after

>   D. Under no circumstances

10.   Personal knowledge of identity along with a government ID would most safely be based on:

>   A. A signer's introduction by a Notary's unsworn, trusted friend

>   B. The fact that a signer is a good business client with excellent credit

>   C. A signer and Notary having two casual acquaintances in common

>   D. A signer's repeated interaction with the Notary over many years.

11.   A notary is authorized to make corrections to a document:

>   A. Only under the direction of an attorney

>   B. As long as all parties to the document are notified

>   C. In any case, unless the document is a will

>   D. Under no circumstances

12.   An oath differs from an affirmation in that:

        A. An oath is a spoken vow; an affirmation is unspoken

        B. An oath makes reference to God; an affirmation does not

        C. Oath-takers are subject to perjury penalties; affirmant are not

        D. An oath requires ceremony; an affirmation does not

13.   In California, notaries are required to maintain errors and omission insurance:

        A. Only in the first year of your commission

        B. Only during your first commission

        C. Notaries are not required to have errors and omission insurance

        D. At all times in order to serve as a notary

14.   California notaries have legal authority to keep copies of all documents that they notarize.:

        A. Only if it involves a deed that effects real property

        B. Only if you are using personal knowledge to notarize the document

        C. Notaries do not have legal authority to keep copies of notarized documents.

        D. Only documents approved by the Secretary of State may be kept.

15.   If your commission is dated April 15, 2016 and you take your oath and file your bond on May 1, 2016, when will your commission expire?

        A. Immediately, because you waited too long to file.

        B. April 30, 2020.

        C. May 1, 2020.

        D. April 14, 2020.

16.   A jurat may not always guarantee that the document signer:

        A. Personally appeared before the Notary

        B. Signed before the Notary

        C. Was given an oath or affirmation by the Notary

        D. Paid a fee to the Notary

17.   When a Notary resigns his or her commission, the journal:

        A. Must be destroyed as soon as possible

        B. Must be surrendered to the county clerk

        C. Must be safeguarded by the Notary's employer in a fireproof file

        D. Must be surrendered to any available Notary

18. **A notary's duties are generally confined to those of a(n):**

    A. Advocate

    B. Agent

    C. Impartial witness

    D. Broker

19. **If a notary is to be removed for misconduct, this will typically be performed by the:**

    A. Secretary of state

    B. Sheriff

    C. Governor

    D. County clerk

20. **Notaries may prepare certified copies of:**

    A. Death certificates

    B. Power of attorney

    C. Birth certificates

    D. College transcripts

21. **The purpose of a notary bond is to:**

    A. Protect the notary from any legal action resulting from his negligence

    B. Protect any person who sustains damage as a result of the notary's improper performance of duty

    C. Authenticate the identity of a notary

    D. Insure the right of subrogation against any party involved in an agreement that proves to be fraudulent of false

22. **Completion of a jurat differs from completion of an acknowledgment in that:**

    A. It involves the administration of an oath

    B. It involves certification as to the identity and execution of the document

    C. The identity of the person appearing must be established

    D. The person's appearance must be voluntary

23. **A notary may NOT take proof of a written instrument by or to a corporation if he:**

    A. Is an employee of the corporation

    B. Is a stockholder of the corporation

    C. Executes the instrument as an individual or representative of the corporation

    D. Executes the instrument as a representative of the corporation

24. **An acknowledgment does not guarantee that the signer:**

    A. Personally appeared before the Notary

    B. Signed the document before the Notary

    C. Was identified by the Notary

    D. Had a valid government issued ID

25. **The primary function of oaths and affirmations is to**

    A. Compel an individual to tell the truth

    B. Compel an individual to identify a signer

    C. Compel an individual to sign document

    D. Compel the Notary to be truthful

26. **A credible witness is used to:**

    A. To identify the signer

    B. Prove that the signer is being truthful

    C. To sign the document for the principal

    D. To sign the document as a witness

27. **The signer of a document isn't required to sign in the presence of a notary for a:**

    A. Acknowledgment

    B. Jurat

    C. Proof of execution

    D. Both A and C

28. **If a notary over charges his constituents he may be subject to:**

    A. A fine

    B. Suspension of his commission

    C. Revocation of his commission

    D. All of the above

29. **Which one of the following documents can be notarized without affixing your notary seal?:**

    A. A Jurat

    B. A grant deed

    C. A California subdivision map

    D. A birth certificate

30. **Once your commission has expired, your notary seal should be:**

    A. Destroyed.

    B. Kept in a locked and secured place that is under the notaries public exclusive control.

    C. Used only until you receive a new authorization to manufacture a seal from the Secretary of State.

    D. All of the above.

EXAMINATION SECTION – TEST 5

DIRECTIONS: Each question or incomplete statement is followed by four possible answers. Select the BEST possible answer or word that completes the question or statement. *CIRCLE THE MOST CORRECT ANSWER.*

1. **Maximum notary fees are set by:**

    A. An agreement between the notary and the constituent

    B. The Secretary of State

    C. California State legislature (Government Code)

    D. There are no maximum fees all fees are negotiable

2. **All of the following are requirements to become a notary EXCEPT:**

    A. Applicant has not been convicted of a felony

    B. Applicant is a citizen of the United States

    C. Applicant is a legal resident of the State of California

    D. Applicant is familiar with duties and responsibilities of a notary

3. **Which of the following would not disqualify an applicant from appointment as a notary public?:**

    A. Legally possessing a handgun

    B. Misconduct

    C. Conviction of a misdemeanor

    D. Conviction of a felony

4. **If your notary journal is stolen and a police report is filed, you must submit notification of the missing journal, to the Secretary of State, which includes**

    A. The period time covered by the journal.

    B. Your notary commission number and expiration date of your commission.

    C. A copy of the police report, if available.

    D. All of the above.

5. **By signing his official signature to the document, the notary _____ to the taking of the acknowledgment:**

    A. Certifies

    B. Agrees

    C. Swears

    D. Grants

6. **The notary's term of office is determined by:**

   A. The date of his commission

   B. The date he passes the exam

   C. His birthdate

   D. The county in which he serves

7. **Of the following, who must be familiar with the practice of a notary public?:**

   A. Notaries

   B. Notaries who are not attorneys

   C. Constituents

   D. Affiants

8. **An affirmation is:**

   A. Is Latin for Jurat.

   B. The legal equivalent of an oath without reference to a supreme being.

   C. Only used when there are three or more affiants.

   D. All of the above.

9. **Notaries generally are authorized to certify a copy of (a):**

   A. A birth certificate

   B. An entry in their notarial journal

   C. A naturalization certificate

   D. A college transcript

10. **Ability to read, write and understand English is:**

    A. Possessed by all U.S. residents

    B. Required of all signers presenting documents to U.S. Notaries

    C. Necessary before entering into a legal contract in the U.S.

    D. Required of applicants for a notarial commission in California

11. **A notary's oath of office is duly executed before:**

    A. The secretary of state

    B. The county clerk, the deputy county clerk or another notary

    C. Any member of the clerk's staff

    D. An attorney

12.   **A notary has authority to act in a county (within the state of California) other than his county of residence:**

A. If he files his oath with the county clerk of another county

B. Only with authorization of the secretary of state

C. At any time

D. At no time

13.   **A notary public's rubber stamp seal should contain each of the following EXCEPT:**

A. Title

B. Commission expiration date

C. State seal

D. Social Security number

14.   **Notaries obtain their authorization to purchase a seal from:**

A.   The Secretary of State.

B.   The County Clerk.

C.   Their local seal manufacturer.

D.   Their employer.

15.   **State of California**

County of _____

Subscribed and sworn to (or affirmed) before me on this _____ day of _____, 20__, by _____, proved to me on the basis of satisfactory evidence to be the person(s) who appeared before me.

Seal_____

Signature_____

The above wording comes from what document?

A. Certificate of acknowledgement

B. Jurat

C. Authentication

D. Affidavit

16. **A notary public who knowingly makes a false certificate at a <u>minimum</u> is guilty of:**

    A. A felony

    B. Plagiarism

    C. A misdemeanor

    D. Fraud

17. **Which of the following is a term used to name a person who makes an affidavit?:**

    A. Advocate

    B. Plaintiff

    C. Witness

    D. Deponent

18. **A document may also be called a(n):**

    A. Declaration

    B. Transcript

    C. Instrument

    D. Certificate

19. **A felony is a(n):**

    A. Indictment

    B. Violation of the law

    C. Crime more serious than a misdemeanor

    D. Crime more serious than malfeasance

20. **When a notary changes his place of residence from one county to another he must notify:**

    A. Only the Secretary of State

    B. The Secretary of State and the county clerk of the new residence

    C. The Secretary of State and the county clerk of the old residence

    D. Both county clerks

21. **The notary's term of office is:**

    A. 1 year

    B. 2 years

    C. 3 years

    D. 4 years

22. **When a subscribing witness brings a document to be notarized, the act is called:**

      A.   Authentication.

      B.   Protest.

      C.   Jurat.

      D.   Proof of execution.

23. **The powers of notaries public are defined by:**

      A. The Secretary of State

      B. Courts of record

      C. Statute

      D. Tradition

24. **Any person WITHOUT an appointment who conveys the impression that he is a notary public may be prosecuted for:**

      A. Misconduct

      B. A Misdemeanor or a felony

      C. Perjury

      D. False advertising

25. **Credible witnesses:**

      A.   Are never placed under oath.

      B.   Must not be named in the document or have a financial interest in the transaction.

      C.   Must always know the notary.

      D.   All of the above.

26. **Which one of your constituent's fingers is the <u>first</u> finger of choice to print in your journal when you are notarizing a deed that affects real property?:**

      A. Right thumb

      B. Left thumb

      C. Right or left index

      D. Any finger is acceptable

27. **A notary must notarize your documents if you have a proper (legal) request and the ability to:**

  A. Pay his or her fees

  B. Produce 2 forms of ID

  C. Show proof of American citizenship

  D. Articulate your needs

28. **Advertising in a foreign language requires that the notary state fees allowed by law in English and:**

  A. French

  B. Spanish

  C. German

  D. The foreign language that the ad is in

29. **The jurisdiction of a California State Notary is:**

  A. The county where your office is located

  B. The entire State of California

  C. The county where the document was created

  D. Northern or Southern California (not both)

30. **If you fail the notary exam the cost to re-take it is:**

  A. Free

  B. $10

  C. $20

  D. $30

EXAMINATION SECTION - TEST 6

DIRECTIONS: Each question or incomplete statement is followed by four possible answers. Select the BEST possible answer or word that completes the question or statement. *CIRCLE THE MOST CORRECT ANSWER.*

1.   **Any person who solicits, coerces, or influences a notary public to improperly maintain the notary's journal is guilty of:**

        A. An infraction

        B. A misdemeanor

        C. A felony

        D. None of the above

2.   **Failure to disclose all arrest and convictions on your application, including dismissed charges, is cause for the Secretary of State to:**

        A. Deny your notary application

        B. Issue a temporary commission (not to exceed 1 year)

        C..Permanent revocation of your commission once discovered

        D. Temporarily suspend your application for a period no less than 1 year

3.   **Which document, when notarized, does not require a seal:**

        A.   Circulator's affidavit.

        B.   Subdivision maps.

        C.   Veterans certificate.

        D.   None of the above, all notarized documents require a seal.

4.   **When using two credible witnesses to establish identity, which of the following statements is true**

        A. The two credible witnesses sign the journal and document

        B. Two credible witnesses may not be used unless the notary personally knows the document signer

        C. Two credible witnesses may be used as long as the notary has a beneficial interest

        D. None of the above

5. **Yolanda was out of town when her commission letter arrived. She missed the deadline for filing her bond and taking her oath. What must she do?**

    A. She must re-apply and re-take her training and state exam

    B. She must re-apply for her commission but does not need to re-take her training or state test

    C. She must re-take her exam only

    D. None of the above

6. **If a notary misplaces his or her notary journal, he or she must submit notification of the missing journal (to the Secretary of State) which includes:**

    A. The period of time covered by your journal entries

    B. Your notary commission number

    C. The expiration date of their notary commission

    D. All of the above

7. **If a notary misplaces his or her notary journal, what should they do?**

    A. Notify the County Clerk and the Secretary of State immediately

    B. Notify the Secretary of State within 30 days via certified mail

    C. Notify the County Clerk within 30 days via certified mail

    D. Notify the Secretary of State immediately via certified mail

8. **What statement is false regarding the notary seal?**

    A. The notary seal may use any color ink that is photographically reproducible

    B. The notary seal may be circular (no more than 2" in diameter).

    C. The notary seal may be retangular (no more than 1" x 1 1/2")

    D. The notary may use an embosser which leaves a raised impression only

9. **The purpose of a surety bond is:**

    A. To protect the state against any monetary awards against the notary

    B. To limit awards against a notary to a maximum of $15,000

    C. To protect the public

    D. To eliminate the need for errors and omissions insurance

10. **A notary is not permitted to translate the term "notary" or "notary public" directly into the Spanish terms "notario" or "notario publico". Violators are subject to the following**

    A. $750 fine and suspension (minimum 6 months) or revocation

    B. $1,500 fine and suspension (minimum 1 year) or revocation

    C. $1,500 fine and suspension (minimum 2 year) or revocation

    D. $1,500 fine and suspension (minimum 3 years) or revocation

11. **If a notary promotes him or herself as an immigration specialist or consultant, advertising themselve as a notary can result in the following action**

    A. A maximum fine of $1,500

    B. Suspension

    C. Revocation

    D. a and b or c

12. **Any member of the public may request a photocopy of a journal entry regarding a notary act provided the written request contains all of the information required by law**

    A. For a fee of $0.30 per page

    B. For a fee of $10.00 per page

    C. For a fee of $20.00 per page

    D. A notary may never provide written information to members of the public

13. **Which of the following statements is true?**

    A. A notary may never notarize a faxed document

    B. A notary may never notarize a document in a language that the notary cannot read or write

    C. A notary may never notarize a birth certificate

    D. A notary may never certifiy a copy of a Power of Attorney

14. **If an award is granted against a notary due to gross negligence or illegal notary actitivities, the notary;**

    A. Is liable for losses up to the amount of his or her bond

    B. Is not liable if a bond has been properly filed with the county clerk

    C. May be required to reimburse the bond company for all losses covered by the bond

    D. Will not be responsible for amounts greater than the face value of the bond

15. **Every notary is required to maintain a journal of official notary acts. This journal is known as a sequential journal because records are entered according to the date and time of service. Which of the following is an acceptable practice?**

    A. A notary may use multiple journals

    B. Complete multiple entries for the same constituient in the same journal

    C. Record information on a date or time that isn't accurate

    D. Record entries for individuals that fail to appear

16. **If a notary falls behind on child support payments, he or she may have their commission**

    A. Suspended or revoked

    B. Suspended or revoked for a period not to exceed 3 years

    C. Will be required to forfeit any fees collected to the Secretary of State

    D. a and c

17. **A notary may be charged with a misdemeanor for willful failure to properly maintain his or her journal. Which of the following would be considered improper maintainence?**

    A. All of the below

    B. Failure to obtain signatures of credible or subscribing witnesses when required

    C. Failure to record the journal entry for a specific notarization

    D. Failure to record the date and time of a notarization

18. **Which of the following statements is false regarding credible witnesses?**

    A. A credible witness may not be a principal to the document

    B. A credible witness may not have a direct beneficial or financial interest in a document

    C. The document signer must always personally know the credible witness

    D. The notary must always personally know the credible witness

19. **When using a credible witness to establish identity, the credible witness:.**

    A. Must swear to the notary that she or he knows the document signer

    B. Must be willing to sign the document and the journal as a credible witness

    C. Must be properly identified and is not required to be personally known by the notary

    D. All of the above

20. **It is illegal for a notary to complete an acknowledgement that contains statements known, by the notary, to be false. Doing so can result in the following penalty(ies)**

    A. State prison or county jail for up to 1 year

    B. State prison for a maximum of 4 years

    C. $750 fine

    D. b and c

21. **In California, a notary is not permitted to:**

    A. Notarize certain immigration documents

    B. Complete any notary act on documents that are in a language other than English

    C. Execute a "power of attorney" certificate

    D. Determine or certify the representative status of an individual

22. **In California, the notary seal must be:**

        A. Photographically reproducible

        B. Used in conjunction with an embossed image wherever the seal appears

        C. Obtained and used by the notary

        D. a and c

23. **The jurat is identified by what wording or phrase?**

        A. Subscribed and sworn (or affirmed) to

        B. Personally appeared

        C. Affidavit

        D. None of the above

24. **An acknowledgement indicates that:**

        A. The signer proved to the notary that she or he is an authorized signer

        B. The document signer personally signed the document in the presence of the notary

        C. The identity of the documents signer was properly verified by the notary

        D. All of the above

25. **According to the Secretary of State, what is the most frequently completed notarial act in California?**

        A. Jurats

        B. Acknowledgements

        C. Completing proofs of execution

        D. Certifications

26. **If a notary decides not to renew his or her commission, they must surrender their journal to the county clerk within 30 days or be subject to a misdemeanor charge:**

        A. A fine up to $750.00

        B. A misdemeanor charge

        C. Financial damages to any party who is injured by the inaction

        D. All of the above

27. **If your journal is lost or stolen, you must notify the Secretary of State within 30 days and include the following information:**

    A. The period of time covered by your journal entries

    B. A copy of the police report, if one was filed

    C. Your notary commission number and commission expiration date

    D. All of the above

28. **A proof of execution may be used for the following document:**

    A. Security agreement

    B. Deed of Trust

    C. Grant Deed

    D. None of the above

29. **When a notary's commission expires, the notary seal should be:**

    A. Kept in a locked area under the direct and exclusive control of the notary

    B. Used until you receive your new seal and then destroyed

    C. Destroyed

    D. Mailed via first class mail to the Secretary of State

30. **A constituient always signs the document and the journal, a subscribing witness always signs**

    A. The document and the journal

    B. The journal only

    C. The document only

    D. A credible witness does not sign the document or the journal

EXAMINATION SECTION

TEST I – ANSWERS

1.C	2.D	3.C	4.A	5.C	6.D	7.A	8.B	9.C	10.A	11.A
12.B	13.A	14.B	15.A	16.D	17.A	18.B	19.D	20.A	21.C	22.A
23.A	24.B	25.D	26.C	27.D	28.D	29.A	30.A			

TEST II – ANSWERS

1.A	2.C	3.C	4.B	5.B	6.A	7.D	8.B	9.C	10.D	11.A
12.C	13.A	14.C	15.B	16.C	17.A	18.D	19.B	20.C	21.D	22.C
23.A	24.D.	25.B	26.A	27.D	28.A	29.A	30.B			

TEST III – ANSWERS

1.B	2.C	3.D	4.A	5.A	6.A	7.A	8.A	9.B	10.D	11.A
12.C	13.A	14.B	15.D	16.A	17.D	18.D	19.B	20.D	21.A	22.D
23.D	24.B	25.D	26.B	27.D	28.D	29.B	30.B			

TEST IV – ANSWERS

1.A	2.D	3.D	4.A	5.B	6.A	7.B	8.D	9.D	10.D	11.D
12.B	13.C	14.C	15.D	16.D	17.B	18.C	19.A	20.B	21.B	22.A
23.A	24.B	25.A	26.A	27.A	28.D	29.C	30.A			

TEST V – ANSWERS

1.C	2.B	3.A	4.D	5.A	6.A	7.A	8.B	9.B	10.D	11.B
12.C	13.D	14.A	15.B	16.C	17.D	18.C	19.C	20.A	21.D	22.D
23.C	24.B	25.B	26.A	27.A	28.D	29.B	30.A			

i

TEST VI – ANSWERS

1.B	2.A	3.B	4.D	5.B	6.D	7.D	8.D	9.C	10.B	11.D
12.A	13.C	14.C	15.B	16.A	17.A	18.D	19.A	20.A	21.D	22.D
23.A	24.C	25.B	26.D	27.A	28.D	29.C	30.A			

Oaths and Affirmations

OATH

Do you solemnly swear that the statements contained herein are true, so help you God?

AFFIRMATION

Do you solemnly affirm, under the penalties of perjury, that the statements made herein are true?

OATH GIVEN TO A SUBSCRIBING WITNESS

Do you solemnly swear that you saw (name of document signer) sign his/her name to the document or heard him or her acknowledge to you that he/she executed it, that you know the signer to be the person he or she claims to be, that he signer asked you to sign as a witness, and that you signed as witness, so help you God?"

IMPORTANT SUMMARY INFORMATION

These are intended as guidelines only.

Acknowledgment Steps

1. Personal Appearance
2. Positive Identification
3. Acknowledge signing the document

Copy Certification

1. Entries of Notary Journal
2. Power of Attorney

Credible Witness(es)

1. Personally knows the signer
2. Takes an oath or affirmation
3. No financial interest or named in document
4. Knows signer does not possess acceptable ID documents
5. Has reasonable belief that it would be difficult or impossible for singer to obtain acceptable ID documents within time frame of transaction
6. If 1 credible witness: is personally known to Notary & valid ID
7. If 2 credible witnesses: identified on the basis of reliable ID documents

Subscribing Witness(es)

1. Never with real estate or security documents
2. Personally know the original signer
3. Signs documents and takes to Notary
4. Subscribing witness must be identified by a credible witness. Credible witness must know subscribing witness and notary public. Credible witness must have satisfactory ID.
5. Takes an oath or affirmation
6. Powers of attorney

Methods of Positive Identification

1. Reliable ID documents
2. 1 personally Known Credible Witness with reliable ID document.
3. 2 unknown Credible Witnesses with reliable ID documents.

Requirements of Reliable ID Documents

1. Be current (or issued within last 5 years)
2. Photograph
3. Physical description
4. Signature
5. Contain serial number

Reliable ID Documents

1. CA Drivers License or CA non-driver ID
2. U.S. Passport
3. Foreign passport (stamped by INS/CIS)
4. Another state's Driver License or non-drivers ID
5. Drivers License issued in Mexico or Canada
6. U.S. Military ID
7. Inmate ID
8. Employee ID issued by federal, state, county or local government

**Non-reliable cards include
Social Security Cards – Credit Cards –
Company ID Cards*

Jurat Steps

1. Personal Appearance
2. Positive Identification
3. Administer oath or Affirmation
4. Sign document in the presence of the Notary

THE TEN COMMANDMENTS

TEN NEVERS A NOTARY NEEDS TO KNOW

NEVER notarize your own signature

NEVER notarize if you are named in the document or have any beneficial or financial interest in the transaction.

NEVER give legal advice by instructing signers on how to complete a document, or advising on anything relating to the document.

NEVER notarize if the signer or oath-taker does not personally appear.

NEVER notarize unless you can identify the signer through a credible witness(es) or reliable identification cards.

NEVER notarize if you are unable to communicate with the signer to determine whether the signature is authentic in the case of an acknowledgment or that the signer swears or affirms to the contents of the document in the case of a jurat.

NEVER sign and seal a document without first completing your journal entries.

NEVER allow a notarial act to go unnoted in your journal. Keep accurate and complete record.

NEVER charge more notary fees than the law allows.

NEVER discriminate in the delivery of your services.

County	Recorder	Street Address	Mailing Address	Phone Number
Alameda	Patrick O'Connell	1106 Madison Street Oakland, CA 94607	Same	(510) 272-6362 (888) 280-7708
Alpine	Doranna Glettig	99 Water Street - Markleeville, CA 96120	P.O. Box 217 Markleeville, CA 96120	(530) 694-2286 (530)-694-2491 fax
Amador	Sheldon Johnson	810 Court Street. Jackson, CA 95642	Same	(209) 223-6468
Butte	Candace Grubbs	25 County Center Drive Oroville, CA 95965	Same	(530) 538-7691
Calaveras	Karen Varni	Government Ctr. - 891 Mtn Ranch Rd. Oroville, CA 95249	Same	(209) 754-6372
Colusa	Kathleen Moran	Courthouse Hall of Records 546 Jay Street Colusa, CA 95932	Same	(530) 458-0500
Contra Costa	Stephen Weir	555 Escobar St. Martinez, CA 94553	P.O. Box 350 Martinez, CA 94553	(510) 646-2955
Del Norte	Vicki Frazier	981 H Street, Suite 160 Crescent City, CA 95531	Same	(707) 464-7216
El Dorado	William E. Schultz	360 Fair Lane Placerville, CA 95667	Same	(530) 621-5495
Fresno	Robert C. Werner	2281 Tulare Street, Room 302 Fresno, CA 93712	P.O. Box 766 Fresno, CA 93712	(209) 488-3471
Glenn	Sheryl Thur	526 W. Sycamore Street Willows, CA 95988	P.O. Box 39 Willows, CA 95988	(530) 934-6412 (530) 934-6305 fax
Humboldt	Carolyn Wilson-Grnich	825-5th Street, 5th Floor Eureka, CA 95501	Same	(707) 445-7382
Imperial	Dolores Provencio	940 Main Street, Room 202 El Centro, CA 92243	Same	(760) 482-4272
Inyo	Mary A. Roper	168 North Edwards Street Independence, CA 93526	P.O.Drawer F Independence, CA 93526	(760) 878-0222 (760) 878-1805 fax
Kern	Jim Fitch	1655 Chester Avenue Bakersfield, CA 93301	Same	(605) 861-2181
Kings	Joan L. Bullock	1400 W. Lacey Blvd Hanford, CA 93230	Same	(559) 582-3211 X2470
Lake	Douglas W. Wacker	225 N. Forbes Street Lakeport, CA 95453	Same	(707) 263-2293
Lassen	Julie Bustamante	220 So. Lassen Street Susanville, CA 96130	Same	(530) 251-8234
Los Angeles	Conny McCormack	12400 Imperial Way Norwalk, CA 90650	P.O. Box 1024 Norwalk, CA 90651	(800) 815-2666
Madera	Rebecca Martinez	200 W 4th St Madera, CA 93637-3548	Same	(559) 675-7724
Marin	Joan Thayer	3501 Civic Center Drive, Suite 232 San Rafael, CA 94903	Same	(415) 499-6092
Mariposa	Gary Estep	4962 - 10th Street Mariposa, CA 95338	P.O. Box 35 Mariposa, CA 95338	(209) 966-5719
Mendocino	Susan M. Ranochak	501 Low Gap Road, Suite 1020 Ukiah, CA 95482	Same	(707) 463-4376
Merced	Kent B. Christensen	2222 "M" Street Merced, CA 95340	Same	(209) 385-7627
Modoc	Shannon Hagge	204 South Court Street, Basement Alturas, CA 96101(	Same	(530) 233-6205
Mono	Lynda Roberts	Annex I, 74 School St. Library Bldg 1st Fl. Bridgeport, CA 93517	P.O. Box 237 Bridgeport, CA 93517	(760) 932-5530

166

County	Recorder	Street Address	Mailing Address	Phone Number
Monterey	Stephen Vagnini	168 West Alisal Street, 1st Floor, Salinas, CA 93901	P.O. Box 292 Salinas, CA 93902	(831) 755-5041 (831) 755-5064 fax
Napa	John Tuteur	900 Coombs Street, Room 116 Napa, CA 94559	P.O. Box 298 Napa, CA 94559	(707) 253-4246
Nevada	Gregory Diaz	950 Maidu Avenue Nevada City, CA 95959	Same	(530) 265-1221
Orange	Tom Daly	12 Civic Center Plaza, Room 101 Santa Ana, CA 92701	P.O. Box 238 Santa Ana 92702	(714) 834-2500
Placer	Jim McCauley	2954 Richardson Drive Auburn, CA 95603	Same	(530) 886-5600
Plumas	Kathy Williams	520 W. Main Street Quincy, CA 95971	P.O. Box 10706 Quincy, CA 95971	(530) 283-6218 (530) 283-6155 fax
Riverside	Larry W. Ward	4080 Lemon Street Riverside, CA 92501	P.O. Box 751 Riverside, CA 92502	(951) 486-7000 (800) 696-9144
Sacramento	Craig A. Kramer	600-8th Street Sacramento, CA 95814	P.O. Box 839 Sacramento, CA 95812	((916) 874-6334 (800) 313-7133
San Benito	John R. Hodges	440 Fifth Street, Room 206 Hollister, CA 95023	Same	(408) 636-4029
San Bernardino	Larry Walker	222 West Hospitality Lane San Bernardino, CA 92415-0022	Same	(909) 367-8306
San Diego	David L. Butler	1600 Pacific Hwy., Room 260 San Diego, CA 92101	P.O. Box 1750 San Diego, CA 92112	(619) 238-8158
San Francisco	Phil Ting	875 Stevenson, 3rd Floor San Francisco, CA 94103	Same	(415) 554-5531 (415) 554-5544 fax
San Joaquin	James Johnstone	6 South El Dorado St. 2nd Floor Stockton, CA 95202	P.O. Box 1968 Stockton, CA 95201	(209) 468-3939
San Luis Obispo (	Julie Rodwald	1055 Monterey Street Room D120)San Luis Obispo, CA 93408-3237	Same	(805) 781-5080 (805) 781-1111 fax
San Mateo	Warren Slocum	555 County Center Redwood City, CA 94063-1665	Same	(650) 363-4500 (650) 363-1903 fax
Santa Barbara	Joseph E. Holland	1100 Anacapa Street Santa Barbara, CA 93101	P.O. Box 159 Santa Barbara, CA 93102	(805) 568-2250
Santa Clara	Regina Alcomendras	70 W. Hedding Street, 1st Fl E. Wing San Jose, CA 95110	Same	(408) 299-2481
Santa Cruz	Sean Saldavia	701 Ocean Street, Room 230 Santa Cruz, CA 95060	Same	(861) 454-2800
Shasta	Cris Andrews	1450 Court St., Ste. 208, Redding, CA 96001-1670	Same	(916) 225-5671
Sierra	Heather Foster	100 Courthouse Square Downieville, CA 95936	Same	(916) 289-3295
Siskiyou	Colleen Setzer	510 N. Main Street Yreka, CA 96097	P.O. Box 8 Yreka, CA 96097	(916) 842-8084
Solano	Robert Blechschmidt	580 Texas Street Fairfield, CA 94533	Same	(707) 421-6290
Sonoma	Bernice A. Peterson	585 Fiscal Drive, Room 103F Santa Rosa, CA 95403	P.O. Box 1709; Santa Rosa, CA 94503	(707) 527-2651
Stanislaus	Donna M. Johnston	1021 "I" Street Modesto, CA 95354	Same	(209) 525-5200
Sutter	Lonna B. Smith	433-2nd Street Yuba City, CA 95991	P.O. Box 1555 Yuba City, CA 95992	(916) 822-7134
Tehama	Bev Ross	633 Washington Street, Room 11 Red Bluff, CA 96080	P.O. Box 250 Red Bluff, CA 96080	(916) 527-3350

County	Recorder	Street Address	Mailing Address	Phone Number
Trinity	Dero Forslund	11 Court Street Weaverville, CA 96093	P.O. Box 1215 Weaverville, CA 96093	(530) 623-1215 (530) 623-8398 fax
Tulare	Gregory Hardcastle	221 S. Mooney Blvd., Room 203 Visalia, CA 93291	Same	(559) 636-5050 (559) 740-4329 fax
Tuolumne	Ken Caetano	2 S. Greet Street Sonora, CA 95370	Same	(209) 533-5531
Ventura	James B. Becker	800 S. Victoria Avenue Ventura, CA 93009	Same	(805) 654-2290
Yolo	Freddie Oakley	625 Court Street, Room 801 Woodland, CA 95695	Same	(530) 666-8130 (530)-666-8109 fax
Yuba	Terry A. Hansen	915 8th. St., Suite 107 Marysville, CA 95901	Same	(530) 749-7850

ALABAMA

Office of Notary Official:
Office of Secretary of State
P.O. Box 5616
Montgomery, AL 36103-5616

State Capitol, Room S-105
600 Dexter Ave.
Montgomery, AL 36104

Key Notary Provisions:
Commission Term: 4 Years
Jurisdiction: State or County
Bond: $10,000
Seal: Embosser
Journal: Required

(334) 242-7205

ALASKA

Notary Public Office
Office of the Lieutenant Governor
240 Main Street, Suite 301
Juneau, AK 99801

Key Notary Provisions:
Commission Term: 4 Years
Jurisdiction: Statewide
Bond: $1,000
Seal: Inked Stamp or Embosser
Journal: Recommended

(907) 465-3509

ARIZONA

Office of Notary Official:
Office of Secretary of State Public Services
Division Notary section
1700 W. Washington, 7th Floor (mail)
1700 W. Washington, Suite 103 (walk-in)
Phoenix, AZ 85007-2808

Key Notary Provisions:
Commission Term: 4 Years
Jurisdiction: Statewide
Bond: $5,000
Seal: Inked Stamp
Journal: Required

(602) 542-4758

ARKANSAS

Office of Notary Official:
Office of Secretary of State Notary Division
State Capitol Little Rock, AR 72201-1094

Key Notary Provisions:
Commission Term: 10 Years
Jurisdiction: Statewide
Bond: $7,500
Seal: Inked Stamp or Embosser
Journal: Recommended

(501) 682-3409

CALIFORNIA

Office of Notary Official:
Office of Secretary of State
Notary Public section
P.O. Box 942877 (1500 11th Street, 2nd Floor)
Sacramento, CA 94277-0001

Key Notary Provisions:
Commission Term: 4 Years
Jurisdiction: Statewide
Bond: $15,000
Seal: Inked Stamp
Journal: Required

(916) 653-3595

COLORADO

Office of Notary Official:
Colorado Department of State,
1700 Broadway, Denver,
Suite 300
Denver, CO 80290

Key Notary Provisions:
Commission Term: 4 Years
Jurisdiction: Statewide
Bond: Not Required
Seal: inked Stamp or Embosser
Journal: Required only for
documents affecting title to real property

(303) 894-2200 ext 6409
(303) 869-4871 fax

CONNECTICUT

Office of Notary Official:
Office of Secretary of State
Records & Legislative Services Division
Notary Public Unit
P.O. Box 150470
30 Trinity Street
Hartford, CT 06115-0470

Key Notary Provisions:
Commission Term: 5 Years
Jurisdiction: Statewide

Bond: Not required
Seal: Recommended by state (embosser or inked stamp)
Journal: Recommended

(860) 509-6151

DELAWARE
Office of Notary Official:
Secretary of State
Notary Public section
Townsend Building
401 Federal Street, Suite 4
Dover, DE 19901

Mailing Address:
Secretary of State
Notary Public section
P.O. Box 898
Dover, DE 19903

Key Notary Provisions:
Commission Term: 2-4 Years
Jurisdiction: Statewide
Bond: Not Required
Seal: Not Required
Journal: Not Required

(302) 739-4111

DISTRICT OF COLUMBIA
Office of Notary Official:
Office of Notary Commissions and Authentications
441 4th Street, NW
Room 810S
Washington, DC 20001

Key Notary Provisions:
Commission Term: 5 Years
Jurisdiction: DC
Bond: $2,000
Seal: Embosser
Journal: Required

(202) 727-3117

FLORIDA
Offices of Notary Officials:
Walk-in:
Department of State
Division of Corporations
Apostille Certification
2661 Executive Center Circle
Tallahassee, FL 32301

Mailing Address:
Department of State
Division of Corporations
Apostille Certification
P.O. Box 6800
Tallahassee, FL 32314-6800

Key Notary Provisions:
Commission Term: 4 Years
Jurisdiction: Statewide
Bond: $7,500
Seal: Inked Stamp
Journal: Recommended   (Required for electronic notarization)

(850) 245-6975
(850) 245-6966 fax

GEORGIA
Office of Notary Official:
Georgia Superior Court Clerks' Cooperative Authority
1875 Century Boulevard
Suite 100
Atlanta, Georgia 30345

Key Notary Provisions:
Commission Term: 4 Years
Jurisdiction: Statewide
Bond: Not Required
Seal: Inked Stamp or Embosser
Journal: Required

(404) 327-6023

HAWAII
Office of Notary Official:
Department of Attorney General
425 Queen Street
Honolulu, HI 96813

Key Notary Provisions:
The Notary's official seal must include: The name of the Notary, the Notary's commission number and the words "Notary Public and "State of Hawaii."

The seal must be circular, not over 2 inches in diameter, and have a "serrated or milled edge border." The seal may still be either an inking stamp or an embosser. Rectangular seals are no longer allowed.

(808) 586-1218

IDAHO
Office of Notary Official:
Office of Secretary of State
Notary Department
PO Box 83720
450 N 4th Street
Boise ID 83720-0080

Key Notary Provisions:
Commission Term: 6 Years
Jurisdiction: Statewide
Bond: $10,000
Seal: Inked Stamp or Embosser
Journal: Recommended

(208) 332-2810

ILLINOIS
Office of Notary Official:
Office of Secretary of State
Index Department
Notary section
213 State Capitol
Springfield, IL 62756

Key Notary Provisions:
Commission Term: 4 Years
Jurisdiction: Statewide
Bond: $5,000
Seal: Inked Stamp
Journal: Recommended by state

(800) 252-8980

INDIANA
Office of Notary Official:
Office of Secretary of State
Notary Department
302 W. Washington Street
Room E018
Indianapolis, IN 46204

Key Notary Provisions:
Commission Term: 8 Years
Jurisdiction: Statewide
Bond: $5,000
Seal: Inked Stamp or Embosser
Journal: Not Required

(317) 232-6542

IOWA
Office of Notary Official:
Office of Secretary of State

Business Services Division
First Floor, Lucas Building
321 E. 12th St.
Des Moines, IA 50319

Key Notary Provisions:
Commission Term: 3 Years
Jurisdiction: Statewide
Bond: Not Required
Seal: Not Required
Journal: Recommended by the state

(515) 281-5204

KANSAS
Office of Notary Official:
Office of Secretary of State
Notary Clerk
Memorial Hall, 1st Floor
120 SW 10th Avenue
Topeka, KS 66612-1594

Key Notary Provisions:
Commission Term: 4 Years
Jurisdiction: Statewide
Bond: $7,500
Seal: Inked Stamp or Embosser
Journal: Recommended by the state

(785) 296-4564

KENTUCKY
Office of Notary Official:
Office of the Secretary of State
Notary Branch
PO Box 821
700 Capital Avenue, Suite 86
Frankfort, KY 40601

Key Notary Provisions:
Commission Term: 4 Years
Jurisdiction: Statewide/Countywide
Bond: Varies per County
Seal: Not Required
Journal: Recommended   (Required for Protests)

(502) 564-3490

LOUISIANA
Office of Notary Official:
Office of Secretary of State
Notary Department
8585 Archives Avenue
Baton Rouge, LA 70809

P. O. Box 94125
Baton Rouge, LA 70804-9125

Key Notary Provisions:
Commission Term: Life
Jurisdiction: Parish wide/Attorneys Statewide
Bond: $10,000/Attorneys Exempt
Seal: Not Required
Journal: Required in Orleans Parish until 12/31/2008

(225) 922-0507
(225) 922-2650 fax

MAINE
Office of Notary Official:
Department of Secretary of State
Bureau of Corporations, Elections and Commissions
Notary Public section
101 State House Station
Augusta, ME 04333-0101

MAINE cont'd
Key Notary Provisions:
Commission Term: 7 Years
Jurisdiction: Statewide
Bond: Not Required
Seal: Not Required
Journal: Required to keep a record of all marriages performed. Journal record of all notarial acts strongly recommended by state.

(207) 624-7736
(207) 287-5874 fax

MARYLAND
Office of Notary Official:
Office of Secretary of State
Notary Division
16 Francis Street,
Annapolis, MD 21401

Key Notary Provisions:
Commission Term: 4 Years
Jurisdiction: Statewide
Bond: Not Required
Seal: Inked Stamp or Embosser
Journal: Required

(410) 260-3860

MASSACHUSETTS
Offices of Notary Officials:
Secretary of Commonwealth Room 1719
Commissions One Ashburton Place
Boston, MA 02108

Key Notary Provisions:
Commission Term: 7 Years
Jurisdiction: Statewide
Bond: Not Required
Seal: Rubber stamp or embosser required
Journal: Required

(617) 727-9640
(617) 742-4538 fax

MICHIGAN
Office of Notary Official:
Michigan Department of State,
Lansing, MI 48918

Key Notary Provisions:
Commission Term: 6-7 Years
Jurisdiction: Statewide
Bond: $10,000
Seal: Not Required
Journal: Recommended

(888) SOS-MICH; (888) 767-6424

MINNESOTA
Office of Notary Official:
Department of Commerce
Office of the Secretary of State
Notary Public
Retirement Systems of MN Building
60 Empire Drive, Suite 100
St. Paul, MN 55103

Key Notary Provisions:
Commission Term: 5 Years
Jurisdiction: Statewide
Bond: Not Required
Seal: Inked Stamp
Journal: Recommended

(651)-296-2803
(877) 551-6767 toll free

MISSISSIPPI
Office of Notary Official:
Office of Secretary of State
700 North Street
Jackson, MS 39202-3024

Mailing:
PO Box 1020
Jackson MS 39215-1020

Key Notary Provisions:
Commission Term: 4 Years

Jurisdiction: Statewide
Bond: $5,000
Seal: Inked Stamp or Embosser
Journal: Required

(601) 359-1499

MISSOURI
Office of Notary Official:
Office of Secretary of State
Commission Division
P.O. Box 784
Jefferson City, MO 65102-0784

Key Notary Provisions:
Commission Term: 4 Years
Jurisdiction: Statewide
Bond: $10,000
Seal: Inked Stamp or Embosser
Journal: Required

(866) 223-6535 toll free
(573) 751-2783
(573)751-8199 fax

MONTANA
Office of Notary Official:
Office of Secretary of State
Notary section
P.O. Box 202801
State Capitol
Helena, MT 59620-2801

MONTANA cont'd
Key Notary Provisions:
Commission Term: 4 Years
Jurisdiction: Statewide
Bond: $10,000
Seal: Inked Stamp or Embosser
Journal: Recommended by the state

(406) 444-1877

NEBRASKA
Office of Notary Official:
Office of Secretary of State
Notary Division
State Capitol, Room 1301
Lincoln, NE 68509
P.O. Box 95104
Lincoln, NE 68509-4608

Key Notary Provisions:
Commission Term: 4 Years

Jurisdiction: Statewide
Bond: $15,000
Seal: Rubber or mechanical stamp
Journal: Recommended by the state

(402)471-2558;
(402)471-4429 fax

NEVADA
Office of Notary Official:
Office of Secretary of State
Notary Division
101 N. Carson Street, Suite 3
Carson City, NV 89701-4786

Key Notary Provisions:
Commission Term: 4 Years
Jurisdiction: Statewide
Bond: $10,000
Seal: Rubber or mechanical stamp
Journal: Required

(775) 684-5708
(775) 684-7141 fax

NEW HAMPSHIRE
Office of Notary Official:
Office of Secretary of State
State House, Room 204
107 North Main Street
Concord, NH 03301

Key Notary Provisions:
Commission Term: 5 Years
Jurisdiction: Statewide
Bond: Not Required
Seal: Inked Stamp or Embosser
Journal: Recommended

(603) 271-3242

NEW JERSEY
Office of Notary Official:
Department of State
Notary Division
33 West State Street, 5th Floor
Trenton, NJ 08608-1214

Key Notary Provisions:
Commission Term: 5 Years
Jurisdiction: Statewide
Bond: Not Required
Seal: Not Required
Journal: Recommended by the state

(609) 530-6421

NEW MEXICO

Office of Notary Official:
Office of Secretary of State
Operations Division
New Mexico State Capitol
325 Don Gaspar, Suite 300
Santa Fe, NM 87503

Key Notary Provisions:
Commission Term: 4 Years
Jurisdiction: Statewide
Bond: $10,000
Seal: Inked Stamp or Embosser
Journal: Recommended by state for all notarizations;
required by law for protests.

(505) 827.3600
(505) 827.3634 fax
(800) 477.3632 toll free

NEW YORK

Office of Notary Official:
Office of Secretary of State, Department
State Division of Licensing Services
Alfred E. Smith Office Building
80 S. Swan Street, 10th floor
Albany, NY 12210
P.O. Box 22001
Albany, NY 12201-2001

Key Notary Provisions:
Commission Term: 2 Years
Jurisdiction: Statewide
Bond: Not Required
Seal: Not Required
Journal: Not Required

(518) 474-4429

NORTH CAROLINA

Office of Notary Official:
Department of Secretary of State
Notaries Division
2 South Salisbury St
Raleigh NC 27601-2903
P.O. Box 29626
Raleigh, North Carolina 27626-0626

Key Notary Provisions:
Commission Term: 5 Years
Jurisdiction: Statewide
Bond: Not Required

Seal: Inked Stamp or Embosser
Journal: Not Required

(919) 733-3406

NORTH DAKOTA

Office of Notary Official:
Office of Secretary of State, Capitol
Building, 600 E. Boulevard Avenue
Bismarck, ND 58505-0500

Key Notary Provisions:
Commission Term: 6 Years
Jurisdiction: Statewide
Bond: $7,500
Seat: Inked Stamp or Embosser
Journal: Recommended by the state

(701) 328-4284
(800) 352-0867 ext. 8-4284 toll free
(701) 328-2992 fax

OHIO

Office of Notary Official:
Ohio Secretary of State
180 E. Broad St., Suite 103
Columbus, OH 43215
Notary Commission Clerk
Ohio Secretary of State
P.O. Box 1658
Columbus, OH 43216-1658

Key Notary Provisions:
Commission Term: 5 Years
Jurisdiction: Statewide
Bond: Not Required
Seal: Inked Stamp or Embosser
Journal: Required for recording protests,
recommended for all notarial acts.

(614) 644-4559
(614) 466-2566
(614) 644-8820 fax

OKLAHOMA

Office of Notary Official:
Office of Secretary of State
Notary Public Division
2300 N. Lincoln, #101
Oklahoma City, OK 73105

OKLAHOMA cont'd
Key Notary Provisions:
Commission Term: 4 Years

Jurisdiction: Statewide
Bond: $1,000
Seal: Inked Stamp or Embosser
Journal: Required

(405) 521-3911 (Form Requests)
(405) 521-2516 (Questions)
(405) 522-3555 (Fax)

OREGON
Office of Notary Official:
Office of Secretary of State
Corporation Division
Notary Public section
255 Capitol Street, N.E., Suite 151
Salem, OR 97310-1327

Key Notary Provisions:
Commission Term: 4 Years
Jurisdiction: Statewide
Bond: Not Required
Seal: Inked Stamp
Journal: Recommended by the state

(503) 986-2200

PENNSYLVANIA
Office of Notary Official:
Department of State, Bureau of Commissions
Elections and Legislation Notary Division
304 North Office Building
Harrisburg, PA 17120

Key Notary Provisions:
Commission Term: 4 Years
Jurisdiction: Statewide
Bond: $3,000
Seal: Inked Stamp & Embosser
Journal: Required

(717) 787-5280
(503) 986-2300 Notary Public Fax

PUERTO RICO
Office of Notary Official:
Supreme Court of Puerto Rico
Office of Notarial Inspection
Ponce de Leon Avenue, #572
Stop 35 1/2 (P.O. Box 190860)
San Juan, PR 00919-0860

Key Notary Provisions:
Commission Term: Life
Jurisdiction: Commonwealth

Bond: $15,000
Seal: Inked Stamp or Embosser
Journal: Not Required

(787)-751-7780

RHODE ISLAND
Office of Notary Official:
Office of Secretary of State
Notary Public Division
148 W. River Street
Providence, RI 02904-2615

Key Notary Provisions:
Commission Term: 4 Years
Jurisdiction: Statewide
Bond: Not Required
Seal: Recommend
Journal: Not Required

(401) 222-3040

SOUTH CAROLINA
Office of Notary Official
Office of Secretary of State
Notary Public Division
Edgar Brown Building
1205 Pendleton Street Suite 525
Columbia, SC 29201
P.O. Box 11350

Columbia, SC 29211

Key Notary Provisions:
Commission Term: 10 Years
Jurisdiction: Statewide
Bond: Not Required
Seal: Embosser
Journal: Not Required

(803) 734-2119

SOUTH DAKOTA
Office of Notary Official:
Office of Secretary of State
Notary Public Division
500 East Capitol, #204
Pierre, SD 57501-5077

Key Notary Provisions:
Commission Term: 6 Years
Jurisdiction: Statewide
Bond: $5,000
Seal: Inked Stamp or Embosser
Journal: Recommended by the state

(South Dakota cont'd)
(605) 773-3539

TENNESSEE
Office of Notary Official:
148 W. River Street
Providence, RI 02904-2615

Key Notary Provisions:
Commission Term: 4 Years
Jurisdiction: Statewide
Bond: $10,000
Seal: Inked Stamp or Embosser
Journal: Required

(615) 741-3699

TEXAS
Office of Notary Official:
Office of Secretary of State
Notary Public Unit, P.O. Box 13375
Austin, Texas 78711 3375

Key Notary Provisions:
Commission Term: 4 Years
Jurisdiction: Statewide
Bond: $10,000
Seal: Inked Stamp or Embosser
Commission Term: 10 Years
Jurisdiction: Statewide
Bond: Not Required
Seal: Inked Stamp
Journal: Required

(512) 463 5705

UTAH
Office of Notary Official:
Utah State Capitol,
Notary Office, Suite 220,
Salt Lake City, UT 84114

Key Notary Provisions:
Commission Term: 4 Years
Jurisdiction: Statewide
Bond: $5,000
Seal: Purple-inked stamp
Journal: Recommended by the state

(801) 538-1041,
(801) 538-1133 fax

VERMONT
Office of Notary Official:
Chittenden Superior Court
175 Main Street,

Burlington, VT 05401

Key Notary Provisions:
Commission Term: 4 Years
Jurisdiction: Statewide
Bond: Not Required
Seal: Not Required
Journal: Recommended by the state

(802) 863-3467

VIRGINIA
Office of Notary Official:
Office of Secretary of Commonwealth
Notary Public Division
P.O. Box 1795
Richmond, VA 23214-1795

Key Notary Provisions:
Commission Term: 4 Years
Jurisdiction: Statewide
Bond: Not Required
Seal: Required
Journal: Not Required

(804) 786-2441

VIRGIN ISLANDS
Office of Notary Official:
Office of the Lieutenant Governor
18 Kongens Gade
St. Thomas, VI 00802

Key Notary Provisions:
Commission Term: 4 Years
Jurisdiction: Virgin Islands
Bond: $5,000
Seal: Embosser
Journal: Required

(340) 774-2991

WASHINGTON
Office of Notary Official:
Department of Licensing
Notaries Public Unit
Department of Licensing
PO Box 9048
Olympia, WA 98507-9048

Key Notary Provisions:
Commission Term: 4 Years
Jurisdiction: Statewide
Bond: $10,000
Seal: Inked Stamp or Embosser
Journal: Not Required

(360) 664-1550
(360) 570-7053 fax

WEST VIRGINIA
Office of Notary Official:
Office of Secretary of State
Notary Public Division
State Capitol, Building 1, Suite 157K
1900 Kanawha Boulevard, East
Charleston, WV 25305-0775

Key Notary Provisions:
Commission Term: 10 Years
Jurisdiction: Statewide
Bond: Not Required
Seal: Inked Stamp
Journal: Required

(304) 558-6000

WISCONSIN
Office of Notary Official:
Office of Secretary of State
P.O. Box 7848
Madison, WI 53707-7848

Key Notary Provisions:
Commission Term: 4 Years
Jurisdiction: Statewide
Bond: $500
Seal: Inked Stamp or Embosser
Journal: Recommended by the state
30 West Mifflin, 10th Floor
Madison, WI 53703

(608) 266-5594

WYOMING
Office of Notary Official:
Notary Division
State Capitol Building
200 West 24th Street
Cheyenne, WY 82002-0020

Key Notary Provisions:
Commission Term: 4 Years
Jurisdiction: Statewide
Bond: $500
Seal: Inked Stamp or Embosser
Journal: Recommended by the state

(307) 777-7378

52298651R00109

Made in the USA
San Bernardino, CA
16 August 2017